# THE ETERNAL PITY

# THE
# ETERNAL PITY

*Reflections on Dying*

*Edited by*

RICHARD JOHN NEUHAUS

UNIVERSITY OF NOTRE DAME PRESS

Notre Dame, Indiana

Copyright 2000 by
University of Notre Dame Press
Notre Dame, IN  46556
All Rights Reserved
Manufactured in the United States of America

A record of the Library of Congress Cataloging-in-Publication Data is available
upon request from the Library of Congress.

ISBN 0-268-02756-0 (cloth)
ISBN 0-268-02757-9 (paper)

The paper used in this publication meets the minimum
requirements of the American National Standard for Information
Sciences—Permanence of Paper for Printed Library Materials,
ANSI Z39.48-1984.

# THE ETHICS OF EVERYDAY LIFE
## Preface to the Series

This book is one of a series of volumes devoted to the ethics of everyday life. The series has been produced by a group of friends, united by a concern for the basic moral aspects of our common life and by a desire to revive public interest in and attention to these matters, now sadly neglected. We have met together over the past five years, under the auspices of the Institute of Religion and Public Life and supported by a generous grant from the Lilly Endowment. We have been reading and writing, conversing and arguing, always looking for ways to deepen our own understanding of the meaning of human life as ordinarily lived, looking also for ways to enable others to join in the search. These anthologies of selected readings on various aspects of everyday life—courting and marrying, teaching and learning, working, leading, and dying—seem to us very well suited to the task. This preface explains why we think so.

We begin by remembering that every aspect of everyday life is ethically charged. Nearly everything that we do, both as individuals and in relations with others, is colored by sentiments, attitudes, customs, and beliefs concerning "how to live." At work or at play, in word or in deed, with kin or with strangers, we enact, often unthinkingly and albeit imperfectly, our ideas of what it means to live a decent and worthy life. Notions and feelings regarding better and worse, good and bad, right and wrong, noble and base, just and unjust, decent and indecent, honorable and dishonorable, or human and inhuman always influence the way we speak to one another, the way we do our work, the way we control our passions, rear our children, manage our organizations, respond to injustice, treat our neighbors, teach the young, care for the old, court our beloved, and face our deaths.

For many centuries and up through the early part of the twentieth century, there was in the West (as in the East) a large and diverse literature on "living the good life," involving manners, patterns of civility, and the meaning of decency, honor, and virtue as these are manifested in daily life. Moralists, both philosophical and religious, wrote voluminously on the moral dimensions of the life cycle (e.g., growing up and coming of age, courting and marrying, rearing the young, aging and dying); on the virtues of everyday life (e.g., courage, endurance, self-command, generosity, loyalty, forbearance, modesty, industry, neighborliness, patience, hope, forgiveness, repentance); on the moral passions or sentiments (e.g., shame, guilt, sympathy, joy, envy, anger, awe) and their proper expression; on the activities of everyday life (e.g., loving, working, caring, giving, teaching, talking, eating); and on basic moral phenomena (e.g., responsibility, obligation, vocation, conscience, praise and blame). These topics, which once held the attention of great thinkers like Aristotle, Erasmus, and Adam Smith, are now sorely neglected, with sorry social consequences.

The ethics of everyday life have been left behind despite—or perhaps because of—the burgeoning attention given these past few decades to professional ethics and public ethics. Mention ethics today, and the discussion generally turns to medical ethics, legal ethics, journalistic ethics, or some other code of behavior that is supposed to guide the activities of professionals. Or it turns to the need to establish codes of conduct to address and curtail the mischief and malfeasance of members of Congress, generals, bureaucrats, or other public officials. In both cases, the concern for ethics is largely instrumental and protective. The codes are intended to tell people how to stay out of trouble with their professional colleagues and with the law. The latter is especially important in a world in which it is increasingly likely that a challenge or disagreement will be engaged not by civil conversation but by an uncivil lawsuit.

Today's proliferation of codes of ethics, while an expression of moral concern, is at the same time an expression of moral poverty. We write new rules and regulations because we lack shared customs and understandings. Yet the more we resort to such external and contrived codes, the less we can in fact take for granted. "Ethics" and "morality" have their source in "ethos" and "mores," words that refer to the ways and attitudes, manners and habits, sensibilities and customs that shape and define a community. Communities are built on shared understandings, usually tacitly conveyed, not only of what is right and wrong or good and bad, but also of who we are, how we stand, what things mean. These matters are not well taught by ethics codes.

Neither are they communicated, or even much noticed, by the current fashions in the academic study and teaching of ethics or by the proliferating band of professional ethicists. The dominant modes of contemporary ethical discourse and writing, whether conducted in universities or in independent ethics centers, are, by and large, highly abstract, analytically philosophic, interested only in principles or arguments, often remote from life as lived, divorced from the way most people face and make moral decisions, largely deaf to questions of character and moral feeling or how they are acquired, unduly influenced by the sensational or extreme case, hostile to insights from the religious traditions, friendly to fashionable opinion but deaf to deeper sources of wisdom, heavily tilted toward questions of law and public policy, and all too frequently marked by an unwillingness to take a moral stand. Largely absent is the older—and we think richer—practice of moral reflection, which is concrete, rooted in ordinary experience, engaged yet thoughtful, attuned to human needs and sentiments as well as to "rational principles of justification," and concerned for institutions that cultivate and promote moral understanding and moral education. Absent especially is the devoted search for moral wisdom regarding the conduct of life—philosophy's original meaning and goal, and a central focus of all religious thought and practice—a search that takes help from wherever it may be found and that gives direction to a life seriously lived.

Many academic teachers of ethics, formerly professors of moral wisdom, are today purveyors of moral relativism. In the colleges and universities ethics is often taught cafeteria style, with multiple theories and viewpoints, seemingly equal, offered up for the picking. But this apparently neutral approach often coexists with ideologically intolerant teaching. Students are taught that traditional views must give way to the "enlightened" view that all views—except, of course, the "enlightened" one—are culture-bound, parochial, and absolutely dependent on your *point*-of-viewing. The morally charged "givens" of human life—e.g., that we have bodies or parents and neighbors—tend to be regarded not as gifts but as impositions, obstacles to the one true good, unconstrained personal choice. Moral wisdom cannot be taught or even sought, because we already know that we must not constrain freedom, must not "impose" morality. Thus, we insist that our "values" are good because we value them, not that they are valued because they are good. Abstract theories of individual autonomy and self-creation abound, while insights into real life as lived fall into obscurity or disappear altogether. To be sure, not all academic teachers of ethics share these opinions and approaches. But experience and study of the literature convinces us that these generalizations are all too accurate.

The current fashions of ethical discourse are of more than merely academic interest. When teachings of "autonomy" or "self-creation" are disconnected from attention to mores and the cultural ethos and from the search for moral wisdom, we come to know less and less what we are supposed to do and how we are supposed to be. Neither can we take for granted that others know what they are supposed to do and be. Being morally unfettered and unformed may make us feel liberated albeit insecure or lost; but seeing that others are morally unfettered and unformed is downright threatening. Thus, despite our moral codes of ethics with penalties attached, despite the boom in the demand for ethicists and in ethics courses in our colleges, our everyday life declines into relationships of narrow-eyed suspicion. No one can argue that we are as a nation morally better off than we were before professional and academic ethics made such a big splash. Americans of widely differing views recognize the growing incivility and coarseness of public discourse and behavior, the sorry state of sexual mores, the erosion of family life, the disappearance of neighborliness, and the growing friction among, and lack of respect for, peoples of differing ages, races, religions, and social classes. To be sure, contemporary ethicists are not responsible for our cultural and moral difficulties. But they have failed to provide us proper guidance or understanding, largely because they neglect the ethics of everyday life and because they have given up on the pursuit of wisdom.

How to provide a remedy? How to offer assistance to the great majority of decent people who still care about living the good life? How to answer the ardent desires of parents for a better life for their children or the deep longings of undergraduates for a more meaningful life for themselves? How to supply an intellectual defense for the now beleaguered and emaciated teachings of decency and virtue? Any answer to these questions depends on acquiring—or at least seeking—a richer and more profound understanding of the structure of human life and the prospects for its flourishing and enhancement. This series of readings on the ethics of everyday life offers help to anyone seeking such understanding.

The topics considered in the several volumes are central to everyday life. Most of us marry, nearly all of us work (and play and rest), all of us lose both loved ones and our own lives to death. In daily life, many of us teach and all of us learn. In civic life, some of us lead, many of us follow, and, in democratic societies, all of us are called upon to evaluate those who would lead us. Yet rarely do we reflect on the nature and meaning of these activities. The anthologized readings—collected from poets and prophets, philosophers and preachers, novelists and anthropologists, scholars and statesmen; from authors ancient, modern, and contemporary—provide rich materials for such reflection. They are moral, not moralistic; they can yield insights, not maxims. The reader will find here no rules for catching a husband, but rather explorations of the purposes of courting and marrying; no prescriptions for organizing the workplace, but competing accounts of the meaning of work; no discussions of "when to pull the plug," but examinations of living in the face of death; no formulae for "effective leadership," but critical assessments of governance in democratic times; no advice on how to teach, but various meditations on purposes and forms of instruction. The different volumes reflect the differences in their subject matter, as well as the different tastes and outlooks of their editors. But they share a common moral seriousness and a common belief that proper ethical reflection requires a "thick description" of the phenomena of everyday life, with their inherent anthropological, moral, and religious colorations.

The readings in this series impose no morality. Indeed, they impose nothing; they only propose. They propose different ways of thinking about our common lives, sometimes in the form of stories, sometimes in the form of meditations, sometimes in the form of arguments. Some of these proposals will almost certainly "impose" themselves upon the reader's mind and heart as being more worthy than others. But they will do so not because they offer simple abstractable ethical principles or suggest procedures for solving this or that problem of living. They will do so because they will strike the thoughtful reader as wiser, deeper, and more true. We ourselves have had this experience with our readings, and we hope you will also. For the life you examine in these pages is—or could become—your own.

Timothy Fuller
Amy A. Kass
Leon R. Kass
Gilbert C. Meilaender
Richard John Neuhaus
Mark Schwehn

To

MILDRED SCHWICH

*for her loving presence through the long watches
of death's vigil*

and

JODY BOTTUM

*for invaluable assistance in putting this book together,
not to mention the gift of Lorena and Little Faith*

# CONTENTS

# INTRODUCTION

1.

Our subject is dying and how we think about dying. It is about the prospect of death, and how we experience the death of others. The subject claims the attention of all thoughtful human beings because we and those we love will surely be claimed by death. "I had not thought death had undone so many," Eliot wrote, echoing Dante. To be precise, death has undone almost all who have gone before us (allowing for a few exceptions proposed by religion and mythology), and our own undoing draws closer with each hour we live. Our subject is not what to do about death, for it is not clear that there is much to be done about it at all. Rather, this discussion and the widely varied readings collected in this book aim at helping us to be more worthily the kind of creatures who will die, and who know they will die.

We are born to die. Not that death is the purpose of our being born, but we are born toward death, and in each of our lives the work of dying is already underway. The work of dying well is, in largest part, the work of living well. Most of us are at ease in discussing what makes for a good life, but we typically become tongue-tied and nervous when the discussion turns to a good death. As children of a culture radically, even religiously, devoted to youth and health, many find it incomprehensible, indeed offensive, that the word "good" should in any way be associated with death. Death, it is thought, is an unmitigated evil, the very antithesis of all that is good.

Death is to be warded off by exercise, by healthy habits, by medical advances. What cannot be halted can be delayed, and what cannot be delayed can be denied. But all our progress and all our protest notwithstanding, the mortality rate holds steady at one hundred percent. Maybe this book will help free the reader from the delusions of progress and the futility of protest. The alternatives to delusion and futility are various, as the authors gathered here will show. In some instances, the alternatives proposed may be no more than alternative delusions and futilities, but that is for the reader to judge.

The readings gathered in this book impose nothing; they only propose. They propose different ways of thinking about death, of encountering death, of being encountered by death—our own death and the death of others. The proposals are often in the form of stories, and some proposals will "impose" themselves upon the reader's mind and heart as being more worthy, more true, than others. But please do not expect ethical principles or equations for resolving the dilemma of death. Be prepared for wisdom. Eliot again: "Where is the Life we have lost in living? Where is the wisdom we have lost in knowledge? Where is the knowledge we have lost in information?" On the far side of wisdom about death, some have found, or found again, the Life that was lost in living against the knowledge that we are creatures who will die, and who know we will die.

2.

Death is the most everyday of everyday things. It is not simply that millions of people die every day, that millions will die this day, although that too is true. Death is the warp and woof of existence in the ordinary, the quotidian, the way things are. It is the horizon against which we get up in the morning and go to bed at night, and the next morning we awake to find the horizon has drawn closer. From the twelfth-century *Enchiridion Leonis* comes the nighttime prayer of children of all ages: "Now I lay me down to sleep, I pray thee Lord my soul to keep; If I should die before I wake, I pray thee Lord my soul to take." Every going to sleep is a little death, a rehearsal for the real thing.

Such is the generality of everyday existence with which the wise have learned to live. But then our wisdom is shattered, not by a sudden awareness of the generality but by the singularity of *a* death—by the death of someone we love with a love inseparable from life. Or it is shattered by the imminent prospect of our own dying. With the cultivated complacency of the mass murderer that he was, Josef Stalin observed, "One death is a tragedy; a million deaths is a statistic." The generality is a buffer against both guilt and sorrow. It is death in the singular that shatters all we thought we knew about death. It is death in the singular that turns the problem of death into the catastrophe of death. In these pages we come across the lamentation of Dietrich von Hildebrand, "I am filled with disgust and emptiness over the rhythm of everyday life that goes relentlessly on—as though nothing had changed, as though I had not lost my precious beloved!"

It used to be said that the Victorians of the nineteenth century talked incessantly about death but were silent about sex, whereas today we talk incessantly about sex and are silent about death. In 1973, Ernest Becker's *The Denial of Death* contended that Freud had gotten it exactly backwards. It is not true, said Becker, that our fear of death is rooted in our denial of sex but, rather, that our fear of sex is rooted in our denial of death. Throughout history, and in many cultures, sex and death have been engaged in a *danse macabre,* and not simply at the shadowed margins of erotic fantasy where dwell the likes of the Marquis de Sade.

In sex and death are joined beginning and ending, the generative and the destructive. In today's culture we chatter incessantly about both sex and death.

They are subjected to the specialization of experts: therapists, ethicists, and the like. Sex and death have been "problematized," and problems are to be "solved" by sexual technique and the technology of dying. Victorian reticence about sex and our former reticence about death may have mystified both, although the probable intent was simply to put them out of mind. In any event, we have now embarked with a vengeance upon a course of demystification. Now there is nothing we cannot talk about in polite company. It is a great liberation. And a great loss, if in fact both sex and death partake of mystery. Mystery is attended by a fitting reticence.

Death and dying has become a strangely popular topic. "Support groups" for the bereaved crop up all over. How to "cope" with dying is a regular on television talk shows. It no doubt has something to do with the growing number of old people in the population. "So many more people seem to die these days," remarked my elderly aunt as she looked over the obituary columns in the local daily. Obituaries routinely include medical details once thought to be the private business of the family. Every evening without fail, at least in our cities, the television news carries a "sob shot" of relatives who have lost someone in an accident or crime. "And how did you feel when you saw she was dead?" The intrusiveness is shameless, and taboos once broken are hard to put back together again.

Evelyn Waugh's *Loved One* brilliantly satirized and Jessica Mitford's *American Way of Death* brutally savaged the death industry of commercial exploitation. Years later it may be time for a similarly critical look at the psychological death industry that got underway in 1969 when Elizabeth Kübler-Ross set forth her five stages of grieving—denial, anger, bargaining, preparatory grief, and acceptance. No doubt many people feel they have been helped by formal and informal therapies for bereavement and, if they feel they have been helped, they probably have been helped in some way that is not unimportant. Just being able to get through the day without cracking up is no little thing. But neither, one may suggest, is it the most important thing. I have listened to people who speak with studied, almost clinical, detail about where they are in their trek through the five stages. Death and bereavement are "processed." There are hundreds of self-help books on how to cope with death in order to get on with life. This book is not one of them.

A measure of reticence and silence is in order. There is a time simply to be present to death—whether one's own or that of others—without any felt urgencies about doing something about it or getting over it. The Preacher had it right: "For everything there is a season, and a time for every matter under heaven: a time to be born, and a time to die . . . a time to mourn, and a time to dance." The time of mourning should be given its due. One may be permitted to wonder about the wisdom of contemporary funeral rites that hurry to the dancing, displacing sorrow with the determined affirmation of resurrection hope, supplying a ready answer to a question that has not been given time to understand itself. One may even long for the *Dies Irae,* the sequence at the old Requiem Mass. *Dies irae, dies illa / Solvet saeclum in favilla / Teste David cum Sibylla:* "Day of wrath and terror looming / Heaven and earth to ash consuming / Seer's and Psalmist's true foredooming."

The worst thing is not the sorrow or the loss or the heartbreak. Worse is to be encountered by death and not to be changed by the encounter. There are pills we can take to get through the experience, but the danger is that we then do not go through the experience but around it. Traditions of wisdom encourage us to stay with death a while. Among observant Jews, for instance, those closest to the deceased observe *shiva* for seven days following the death. During *shiva* one does not work, bathe, put on shoes, engage in intercourse, read Torah, or have one's hair cut. The mourners are to behave as though they themselves had died. The first response to death is to give inconsolable grief its due. Such grief is assimilated during the seven days of *shiva,* and then tempered by a month of more moderate mourning. After a year all mourning is set aside, except for the praying of *kaddish,* the prayer for the dead, on the anniversary of the death.

Milton Himmelfarb's reflection in the pages that follow lifts up the importance of ritual in the face of death. Many people have been mistaught to think that there is something trivial, artificial, and even dishonest about ritual. We speak of "mere" ritual. The important thing, or so we are told, is to concentrate on how we *feel* about what is happening. This attitude has its source in what some philosophers call "modern emotivism," the doctrine that the authenticity and sincerity of our feeling is all that matters. In fact, there is something that might be called "artificial" in ritual in that ritual is an artifact. That is to say, rituals are constructed by communities of people beyond number who have been here before us. Encountered by the singularity of the death of a particular person who had never been here before and will never be here again, we may cry out in our immeasurable sense of loss that precisely *this* catastrophe has never happened before. There is truth in that, but another truth, and what we come to understand in time is a greater truth, is in the ritual that tells us that we are not alone in our aloneness.

### 3.

In a wrenchingly poignant story in these pages, Peter de Vries would call us to "The recognition of how long, how very long, is the mourners' bench upon which we sit, arms linked in undeluded friendship—all of us, brief links ourselves, in the eternal pity." From the pity we may hope that wisdom has been distilled, a wisdom from which we can benefit when we take our place on the mourners' bench. Philosophy means the love of wisdom, and so some may look to philosophers in their time of loss and aloneness. George Santayana (1863–1952) wrote, "A good way of testing the caliber of a philosophy is to ask what it thinks of death." What does it tell us that modern philosophy has had relatively little to say about death? Ludwig Wittgenstein (1889–1951) wrote, "What can be said at all can be said clearly; and whereof one cannot speak thereof one must be silent." There is undoubtedly wisdom in such reticence that stands in refreshing contrast to a popular culture sated by therapeutic chatter. But those who sit, arms linked in undeluded friendship, cannot help but ask and wonder.

All philosophy begins in wonder, said the ancients. With exceptions, contemporary philosophy stops at wonder. We are told: Don't ask, don't wonder, about what you cannot know for sure. But the most important things of everyday life we cannot know for sure. We cannot *know* them beyond all possibility of their turning out to false. We order our loves and loyalties, we invest our years with meaning and our death with hope, not knowing for sure, beyond all reasonable doubt, whether we might not have gotten it wrong. What we need is a philosophy that enables us to speak truly, if not clearly, a wisdom that does not eliminate but comprehends our doubt.

The brave new world of much modern philosophy, which is no longer very new, is strangely silent about death. Death is a surd, an irrational event, that inconveniently disrupts a world that is otherwise under rational control. It is a subject pushed to the side, best left to the specialists of medical and therapeutic technique. The result is a weirdly unreal view of reality, a kingdom of let's-pretend-things-are-not-as-they-are. In the words of Edna St. Vincent Millay:

> Childhood is not from birth to a certain age and at a certain age
> The child is grown, and puts away childish things.
> Childhood is the kingdom where nobody dies.
> Nobody that matters, that is.

Philosophers of the Anglo-American analytic school have tended to suggest that not much can meaningfully be said about death because, by definition, those who are alive do not *know* death in a way that makes it subject to rational analysis. This view is reinforced by a strong prejudice against metaphysics, the exploration of reality beyond what we can learn by measurable experience. Such philosophers are inclined to say with Jesus, but with a very different intention, "Let the dead bury their dead." Not because the question of death is answered in the mystery of God's purposes but because the question is unanswerable. It is a subject best left to novelists, poets, and explorers into the darker regions of the psyche. Other philosophers, such as the German Schopenhauer (1788–1860), have insisted that death is the muse, the source of inspiration, of all philosophy. But it is a muse that hovers mockingly, exposing the limits and, finally, the futility of all we think we know for sure.

For many philosophers ancient and modern, the chief concern is not with understanding death but with tempering or overcoming the fear that death evokes. In his dictionary, Voltaire declared, "The human species is the only one which knows that it will die, and it knows this through experience." There has been much debate over the years over whether some lower animals are aware of their approaching extinction, and whether in some primitive cultures human beings did not live in happy or pitiable obliviousness to the onrush of death. Since it is only our own experience that, in Voltaire's phrase, we know through experience, such questions may never be resolved. In this century, Sigmund Freud wrote very influentially, if somewhat confusedly, about our awareness of death. In his early work, he contended that our consciousness of death is really superficial since our unconscious is firmly convinced of its immortality. In a later period he would write about the myriad ways in which our behavior is driven by an unconscious death wish. So which is it? It is as though the hovering muse were playing hide-and-seek with us.

Philosophers of an earlier time thought they had a firm fix on the location of death. The philosophical goal was to rob it of its sting. Four centuries before Christ, Epicurus declared that the fear of death rested on two mistakes. First, it was thought to be painful, and second, it was thought that the soul might survive to experience punishment in another life. All that had to be done was to expose these mistakes, and then it would be evident, as Epicurus wrote to a friend, that "Death is nothing to us. It does not concern either the living or the dead, since for the former it is not, and the latter are no more." Thus did the Epicureans neatly dispatch death, turning it into nothing more than a pleasant falling asleep.

Not surprisingly, many have found that solution less than satisfactory. For many, a falling asleep into a permanent loss of consciousness is precisely the terror of death. Loss of consciousness is feared as a loss of being. Not being is no solution at all. The twentieth-century Spanish existentialist philosopher Miguel de Unamuno says that "as a youth and even as a child, I remained unmoved when shown the most moving pictures of hell, for even then nothing appeared to me quite so horrible as nothingness itself." In this view, to be in hell is better than not to be at all.

Teaching at the same time as the Epicureans, the Stoics proposed a different solution. The wise man, they said, is freed as much as possible from all sensations of grief or joy, submitting himself entirely to a natural law that included death. The Stoic view keeps reappearing in history, and in this book is very ably represented by the sixteenth-century French essayist Montaigne, who would persuade us that "To Philosophize Is to Learn to Die." That is the approach urged upon Hamlet by his mother when she counsels him that "All that lives must die." Later we will come to Jody Bottum's explanation of why he and so many others find that counsel unconvincing.

To overcome the fear of death, said the Stoics, we have but to think about it constantly. Seneca repeatedly compared death to a banquet from which we should retire graciously at the appointed time, or to a role in a play that should satisfy us when it is over since that is all that the author wrote. Behind this was the view of Plato that philosophizing means learning to die. That may sound dreadfully dour and even macabre, unless it is understood that learning to die means communing with the eternal that never dies. Death is part of Nature with a capital N, which is the providential ordering of reality.

Marcus Aurelius, the noblest of Stoics, wrote, "Remember that no man loseth other life than that which he liveth, nor liveth other than that which he loseth." Whether it is our own death or the death of someone we love, we uselessly agitate ourselves by regretting what was not to be. "The longest-lived and the shortest-lived man, when they come to die, lose one and the same thing." What is there to mourn? In the final analysis, nothing is lost. We can only lose what might have been, and tranquillity comes with the recognition that there is no "might have been." What is is, what was was, and all is as it must be. In current theories of the stages of grief, this is sometimes called "acceptance."

For other thinkers, death is less to be passively accepted than to be defiantly embraced. If you must die—and you must—then flaunt it. "I teach you the Superman," declared Nietzsche in *Thus Spake Zarathustra*. "Man is something that is to be surpassed." "He is a rope stretched between the animal and the Superman—a rope over an abyss." By proudly embracing death as the natural terminus of life, one surpasses the limits of the natural. The ability to forego all consolations is itself a kind of consolation. Rejecting the proud posture of the Superman, yet others adamantly insist that there is no consolation beyond the loss of consolations. Unamuno's childhood nightmare is true: I have not really faced death until I have faced nothingness, and since nothingness is nothing, there is no *I* to face it. Death is not only the obliteration of the self but the nonexistence of the self to be obliterated.

"Our own death," Freud decreed, "is unimaginable." The late Karl Menninger, a psychiatrist, wrote, "It may be considered axiomatic that the human mind cannot conceive of its non-existence." If I think I have succeeded in conceiving my nonexistence, it is still *I* who conceive it and therefore I exist. "Whenever we make the attempt to imagine our death," Freud observed, "we perceive that we survive as spectators." To this line of reasoning it may be objected that we can conceive of our nonexistence before we were conceived in our mother's womb, so why can we not just as readily conceive of our nonexistence when we die? To that it might be answered, in turn, that our nonexistence before we were conceived is not so much nonexistence as not-yet-existence. I know now that the person that was not before I came to be—except possibly as a thought in the minds of our parents or the mind of God—came to be the person that I undeniably am. These are intriguing "thought experiments," although some may be forgiven for thinking that they are little more than playing with puzzles in order to distract our attention from the smashing hammer blow to existence that is death itself.

The idea of death as absolute nothingness—and, oddly enough, as a kind of fulfillment—has been influentially promoted by the disciples of the German philosopher Martin Heidegger (1889–1976) who make a sharp distinction between the death of others and our own dying. "Our death," wrote his American disciple, Peter Koestenbaum, "is generically different from the death of others." If we view the matter in a "phenomenological" way, we see that the death of somebody else is the removal of "an object in the world," but it does not remove "the observing ego or subject." When we consider another's death, we are still in the picture; death is an event within the world, but the world goes on. My own death is a very different matter. When I think that I am thinking about myself being dead, I am deceiving myself, for I have then sneaked myself back into the picture as the observer. The whole point of my being dead is that the observer is eliminated. "With the extinction of the observer, the entire scene vanishes as well." And so it is, says Koestenbaum, that "my image of the death of myself is tantamount to asserting the end of the world." There is no consolation for the end of the world.

This brief excursus on philosophical understandings of death may leave us wondering about Santayana's maxim that "a good way of testing the caliber of a philosophy is to ask what it thinks of death." Much depends, of course, on the caliber or the quality that we are looking for. Are we, for instance, looking for the truth about death or are we looking for ways to cope with what we can never understand? We may think that we can understand the death of others as "an event within the world," but in fact it would seem that we can only understand our experience of others' dying and being dead. Only the other person could understand his own death and, since he is dead and therefore is no more, even he cannot do that. And if death is truly the extinction of the self, I will never understand my own death because, being dead, there is no *I* to understand or to be understood. In our efforts to come to terms with death, it would seem that philosophy offers slim pickings. Little wonder that so many still today fall back on the austere doctrine of the Stoics that what is must be, and therefore our mourning over what might have been is but an indulgence of irrational passion.

4.

Yet most of those who have sat on the long mourners' bench, arms linked in undeluded friendship and contemplating the eternal pity, look to other sources of wisdom. Most commonly they look to sources of wisdom called religious. To the modern skeptic, religion is the fall-back position when philosophy fails. In the absence of truth, religion provides consolation, and in return for consolation one might be prepared to pay the price of delusion. Deluded friendship is still friendship and may be preferred to facing nothingness all alone. The great religions, however, purport to be sources of wisdom. Their teachers, too, are philosophers—"lovers of wisdom"—who are not confined to the cramped dictates of the empirical, of what can be measured and tested in the laboratories of modern science. To paraphrase Hamlet's reproach of Horatio, "There are more things in heaven and earth than are dreamt of in your philosophical seminars or tested by your science."

One assumes that most readers of this book are, to the extent they count themselves as religious, Christians or Jews. So pervasive is the penetration of biblical religion in our culture that even atheists are not generic atheists but Christian or Jewish atheists. That is to say, it is biblical religion that defines what they reject. In recent decades, however, there is an evident fascination with "Eastern religions," albeit frequently imported in forms that are highly westernized. We begin this brief excursus on religion and the understanding of death with Hinduism and Buddhism, then turning to Islam, Judaism, and Christianity. Each claims to offer a comprehensive account of reality, which would not be comprehensive if it did not include the reality of death. Of each we can ask whether it corresponds to our experience—rational, emotional, poetic—of the way things really are, or of the way things believably might be.

In its beginnings more than three thousand years ago, Hinduism concentrated on affirming life and had little to say about death. In the oldest literature, the *Vedas*, death is to be postponed as long as possible, and there is only the vaguest sense of a soul that might survive death. There is, however, a feared "redeath" or "second death" that happens after the death of the body, and this receives extensive elaboration in the *Upanishads*, which are meant to be an interpretation of the earlier sacred texts. The affirmation of life is now severely tempered, falling under the shadow of Atman, the eternal soul that lives in everything but has no personal characteristics. Atman was never born and will never die and, according to one sage, "is concealed in the heart of all beings;

smaller than the smallest atom, greater than the vast spaces." Atman is identical with Brahman, and Brahman is that which is truly real as distinct from the tangible universe (Maya) that only appears to be real.

Because Atman has no beginning and no end, it follows that death is not truly real. In the *Bhagavad Gita* the god Krishna reproaches Prince Arjuna, who is grieving over the friends who will be killed in a coming battle: "The truly wise mourn neither for the living or the dead. There never was a time when I did not exist, nor you, nor any of these kings. Nor is there any future in which we shall cease to be." Unlike the Stoic rejection of mourning, it is here rejected because death is not real, and death is not real because life is not real. Not *really* real. The self that dies is an illusion that is carried along by the laws of a world in which everything is being endlessly changed. Here the dreaded "redeath" of the *Vedas* now reappears as the dreaded rebirth. This gives rise to the doctrine of reincarnation (Samsara) in which the unliberated soul is carried forward by its deeds and their effect (Karma) into other births and other deaths.

The ultimate goal, according to Krishna, is to be freed from "the terrible wheel of death and rebirth." This is not the immortality of the soul but the elimination of all false modes of existence in which the "I" is attached to this concrete and unreal world. The great mistake that chains us to the "terrible wheel" of repeated cycles of life and death and rebirth—whether rebirth as a cockroach, a princess, or any number of other reincarnations—is to think this world is real. Only by acquiring true knowledge can one be liberated from the wheel, and true knowledge cannot mean knowledge about this world, for everything we know about the world is as false as the world itself. True knowledge is the experience in which the difference between subject and object is eliminated and, in perfect detachment from the world, one is united with Atman/Brahman that knows neither birth nor death. "Whoever knows Brahman," says the Mundaka Upanishad, "becomes Brahman."

Such knowledge is not come by easily. In the Upanishads, the method of liberating knowledge is Yoga. In the window of a health club near my Manhattan office is a listing of instructions offered, including "Yoga in easy lessons." It is but one of many instances in which Eastern religion is used to provide a tincture of the exotic in western commerce. The Yoga of the Upanishads is a discipline of great subtlety and difficulty whose masters move through eight levels to the spiritual perfection of Samadhi. At that highest level, all marks of one's personhood are erased and one can neither be born nor die. The union with Atman/Brahman is complete and there is nothing but a deep, dreamless sleep from which one never wakes. The curse of life has been definitively overcome.

Needless to say, such a view is in sharpest contrast to Western understandings of life and death. "Just to be is a blessing. Just to live is holy," wrote the late rabbi and my dear friend Abraham Joshua Heschel. It is with the sardonic wickedness of a westerner intending to shock that Mark Twain said, "Whoever has lived long enough to find out what life is, knows how deep a debt of gratitude we owe to Adam, the first great benefactor of our race. He brought death into the world." On the other hand, if the alternative is endless existence on "the terrible wheel of death and rebirth," one may well view a final death as a benefaction. The tales of reincarnation peddled in our popular culture are told by people who claim that in their former lives they were kings and queens and famous lovers. It seems nobody was a slave or beggar, never mind a lizard or flea. The Hindu teachers who have thought seriously about reincarnation know better.

Almost three hundred million people today follow one version or another of the teachings of Siddhartha Gautama, otherwise known as the Buddha, which means the Enlightened One. The great insight that came to the Buddha six centuries before Christ is that everything is under the power of Dukkha, or suffering. Suffering, in turn, is not caused by something that happens to you but by your desire or craving. Moreover, everything that exists has its origin in something else. All things are caused, nothing is permanent, everything is destined for oblivion. The reason we suffer in this life is that we struggle against the radical impermanence of everything, and most particularly we struggle against death. The only cure is to give up, to yield oneself to oblivion.

In the wakeless sleep of union with Atman, classical Hinduism promises an overcoming of death. Buddhists, on the other hand, teach the achievement of nonself or *anatman*. Rising above all desire for timeless selfhood, one surrenders to the causal flux of everything in a "middle path" that is without suffering. As with Yoga, this is no easy achievement. The main obstacle to such achievement is in our own heads. Our suffering comes from a mental addiction to thinking of ourselves as permanent beings. "All that we are is the result of what we have thought," says the first chapter of the Dhammapada. "It is founded on our thoughts, it is made up of our thoughts. If a man speaks or acts with an evil thought, pain follows him, as the wheel follows the foot of the ox that draws the wagon." We are the victims of the "primacy of mind," and the mind leads us into spiritually destructive falsehoods, the chief of which is that we can avoid death by somehow making life permanent—as in the idea of an immortal soul.

Only the mind can free the mind from these destructive falsehoods. The Buddha remedied his disciples' craving for eternal truths by the "fourfold denial." When asked, for example, whether the holy person continues to exist after death, he answered: A saint exists after death; a saint does not exist after death; a saint both exists and does not exist after death; a saint neither exists nor does not exist after death. To the logical mind of the West, this seems like jibberish. It may also seem like jibberish to the logical mind of the East. In the Buddhist view, the lethal link that must be broken is the mind's attachment to logic. Neither the question nor the answer about life after death is spiritually important; indeed they are obstacles to enlightenment. Death is simply there to be accepted. Any effort to get around death, even in the form of speculation about the meaning of death, can only cause anguish.

In some Buddhist monastic disciplines, the monks are compelled to sit silently in the presence of a corpse in varying stages of decay. After a long period of meditation on the decaying corpse, one learns that death is nothing in itself; and if death is nothing in itself, neither is life. In Zen Buddhism, death plays a role similar to that of a meaningless expression, such as "the sound of one hand clapping." As one concentrates ever more intensely on such a "koan," the mind is emptied of everything else. The emptied mind is incapable of the vain speculations that lead one back to suffering. When death is treated as a koan, it becomes evident that all things, including life and death, are empty, and in this enlightenment all craving for the changeless is terminated in the state of Nirvana, which is perfect extinction, the achievement of *anatman,* the arrival at nonself.

### 5.

For the nearly one billion Muslims in the world, both life and death are very real indeed. Death is portrayed in graphic images that may strike non-Muslims as fantastical, but they perhaps have the merit of cutting through philosophical abstractions. The Qur'an, the sacred book of Islam, has no systematic treatment of death but the clues that it provides are elaborated in the fourteenth-century "Book of the Soul" (*Kitab-al-ruh*). As in all Islamic teaching, the premise on which everything builds is the omnipotence of Allah. (Contrary to common opinion, Allah does not denote a god other than the one we westerners refer to as God. Allah is simply the Arabic word for God.) Allah does everything; he brings people into being, sets the span of their lives, and causes them to die. Everything is determined ahead of time. To use a western and Christian term, Islam teaches a strict doctrine of predestination. Although we cannot read it, the ticket we get at the beginning of life's journey is imprinted with our final destination, and with all the stops along the way.

The very word "Islam" is Arabic for "surrender," and all of life is conceived as unqualified submission to the will of Allah. Not surprisingly, questions of predestination and free will have occupied Muslim thinkers for centuries. If everything is determined ahead of time, for instance, one may ask what purpose there was in the mission of the Prophet Muhammed, or in today's call for people to change their lives. Recognizing some of these intellectual difficulties, the Prophet declared that "only a little knowledge was communicated to man" and it is our duty to submit to what is revealed, not to speculate about what was not revealed. And yet, inevitably, Muslim thinkers have speculated. It is suggested by various authorities, for instance, that there is something like a life spirit or soul (*nafs*) within each human being. This makes possible individuality—why it is that I am not someone else—and explains what we ordinarily call consciousness.

Death is commonly compared with going to sleep, and going to sleep is sometimes called "the little death." While people are sleeping, God takes away their souls. If it is not yet time for someone to die, God returns the soul when the person awakes. In this context, "Now I lay me down to sleep" takes on a very specific meaning, since God both "keeps" and "takes" my soul while I am sleeping. I have in a sense experienced dying as many times as I have experienced going to sleep. If it is really my time to die, the soul "rises into the throat" and thus escapes the body. Modern medical experts have remarked on the compatibility of Muslim teaching with current definitions of death, such as "brain death." For instance, brain stem lesions frequently create breathing disturbances that may easily be associated with something happening in the throat. Notably absent in Islamic thought, and in most medical concepts of death today, is any reference to the function of the heart in defining death.

When someone dies, the Angel of Death (*malak al-mawt*) comes and sits at the head of the deceased and tells the soul its destination. Wicked souls are told "to depart to the wrath of God," whereat they try to run away by seeking refuge in various parts of the body. Such souls must then be extracted "like the dragging of an iron skewer through moist wool, tearing the veins and sinews." This explains the frequently anguishing death throes to which many are subjected. After getting the soul out of the body, angels place it in a hair cloth and "the odor from it is like the stench of a rotting carcass." After a complete account of sins is made, the soul is returned to the body in the grave. Righteous souls, on the other hand, are told to depart to the mercy of God and they leave the body, "flowing as easily as a drop from a waterskin." Angels wrap such souls in a perfumed shroud and they are taken to "seventh heaven" for a time before being returned to their bodies.

A blue angel (Munkar) and a black angel (Nakir) then question the deceased about the basic teachings of Islam. Unbelievers who fail this test at the grave are tormented by terrible heat and smoke that are let into the grave from *jihannam* (hell), and the grave itself contracts painfully "so that their ribs are piled up upon one another." And so it continues until the final judgment when both believers and unbelievers are raised up and given physical bodies with which they can either enjoy or suffer what awaits them. The righteous enter the Garden of Delights, which are described in very palpable terms of sensual

pleasure, whereas unbelievers at the Day of Judgment are forced to bloat themselves with bitter fruit and "drink down upon it hot water, drinking as drinks
the camel crazed with thirst." After that, they are sent off to hell where they
put on "garments of fire" and have boiling water poured over their heads. This
goes on endlessly, for annihilation is ruled out. Allah declares that "whenever
their skins are cooked to a turn, We shall substitute new skins for them, that
they may feel the punishment."

A very special and enviable fate is reserved for the martyrs of Islam who
die in a *jihad*—a struggle for truth commonly called a "holy war." Anything
they have done wrong in their lives is immediately expiated by their holy death
and the formalities of judgment are dispensed with. They immediately enter
the Garden of Delights. The Shiites, followers of the smaller of Islam's two
major branches, have developed a special zeal for martyrdom, perhaps because
the slaughter of the Prophet's grandson, Husayn, in 680 played a central part
in the origins of the Shiite movement. Today, especially in the Middle East,
some Islamic teachers complain that martyrdom has been cheapened by be-
stowing the title of martyr on almost anyone who died in a state of hostility
to Islam's enemies, notably the State of Israel. It should be noted also that some
Muslim thinkers, influenced by the mystic tradition of the Sufis, have treated
the more graphic details in the teaching as metaphorical, and, against a rigid
determinism, have emphasized more strongly the dimension of individual responsibility.

The Muslim view of death, as of life, is uncompromisingly earthy and concrete, allowing for no evasion of the reality of what is experienced as real. Angelic interventions and other impositions on reality notwithstanding, the facts
of death and putrefaction are accorded great respect. Cremation of the body
is unthinkable, and medical students can only study anatomy using cadavers
of non-Muslims, who are already damned in any case. This extends to strong
inhibitions about organ transplants. Liver transplants are prohibited because
the Prophet's uncle, Hamzah, was murdered by a heathen who opened his belly
and chewed up his liver. Kidney transplants are another matter, however. Since
the Hadith (sayings attributed to the Prophet) makes it clear that those enter-
ing the Garden of Delights will never have to urinate, the removal of the kid-
neys is thought to be no great loss.

### 6.

The understanding of death in Judaism necessarily engages Christian
teaching as well, since the latter depends upon and emerges from the former.
As St. Paul writes in Romans 12, Christians are like branches grafted on to the

root of Israel. He urges Christians to "remember it is not you that support the root, but the root that supports you." But first we will treat the Jewish understanding of death, and then turn to the development of that understanding in Christianity. The first thing to be said about death in this context is that it is not natural. Death is the result of sin. This is made clear in the creation story of chapters two and three of Genesis. "The Lord God took the man and put him in the garden of Eden to till it and keep it. And the Lord God commanded the man, saying, 'You may freely eat of every tree of the garden; but of the tree of the knowledge of good and evil you shall not eat, for in the day that you eat of it you shall die.'"

Interpreters of this passage are by no means of one mind about its meaning. One view is that "the fall" in the garden was really, so to speak, a fall up rather than down. That is to say, Adam and Eve lived in the garden as little more than innocent animals until they ate of the tree of the knowledge of good and evil. With that transgression, they lost immortality but gained the consciousness that we associate with being fully human. Alternatively, it said that before the transgression they lived in perfect communion with God and what God willed. The transgression consisted not in gaining a knowledge of good and evil but in presuming to know on their own and to decide on their own what is good and what is evil. The transgression was, as it were, a declaration of independence from God.

Similarly, there is disagreement about whether death should be understood as a punishment for sin or simply as a result of sin. In the latter case, the statement that "in the day that you eat of it you shall die" is simply a warning about the consequences of doing what is forbidden. In any event, death is not part of the natural created order that God declared to be good. With death came other consequences: exile from the garden, the pain of childbirth, and a life of onerous labor. Adam and Eve are driven out of paradise into death, but also into history. From here on in the Jewish tradition, there is an unbreakable connection between death and history.

In the Hebrew Bible that Christians call the Old Testament, Yhwh again and again rescues his people, but he always rescues them for history, not from history. There is nothing here comparable to the Platonic idea—an idea evident also in some strands of Christian thought—that the immortal soul will survive death. Yhwh's promise to Abraham, for instance, is not that he will be rewarded with immortality but that his tribe will be multiplied. "I will make your descendants as the dust of the earth; so that if one can count the dust of the earth, your descendants also can be counted" (Genesis 13:16). In the Bible, the dead are mourned, and suffering Job can cry out that he hates life, but Yhwh's response is not to eliminate death. Rather, he again and again saves them from their enemies so that their history will continue. Yhwh leads Israel out of bondage in Egypt to a promised land that renews history, not to a deathless kingdom of the Garden of Eden restored.

At least in the early periods of the Jewish tradition, there is no confidence that the soul will survive death. The Psalms and other parts of the Bible speak often of "Sheol," but it seems that Sheol is neither heaven nor hell but simply a shadowy realm where the dead dwell. It seems that nothing happens there. Sheol is not so much an after-life as an after-death. "For in death there is no remembrance of thee; in Sheol who can give thee praise?" (Psalm 6:5). Of the foolish it is said, "Like sheep they are appointed for Sheol; Death shall be their shepherd; straight to the grave they descend, and their form shall waste away; Sheol shall be their home." Then the Psalmist immediately adds, "But God will ransom my soul from the power of Sheol, for he will receive me." (Psalm 49:14–15)

The last sentence is one of many intimations of immortality in the Bible that later Judaism will develop further. In Jewish-Christian dialogue today it is commonly said that Christianity is concerned about the salvation of the soul whereas Judaism's concern is for the redemption of the world. In fact, the two concerns are not unrelated, and certainly not antithetical. Especially after the biblical period, Jews increasingly regard the soul as immortal, and the vindication of the righteous dead becomes an integral part of the world's redemption. This is notably evident in the Talmud, which includes the authoritative interpretations in the Mishnah (the oral teachings given Moses at the same time as the written law) and in the Gemara, which are commentaries on the Mishnah. While the Talmud did not receive its final form until the early centuries of the Christian era, it is clear that the teaching goes back to a much earlier era.

In the Book of Daniel, for example, we find a powerful passage envisioning the resurrection of the dead and a general judgment. "At that time shall arise Michael, the great prince who has charge of your people. And there shall be a time of trouble, such as never has been since there was a nation till that time; but at that time your people shall be delivered, every one whose name shall be found written in the book. And many of those who sleep in the dust of the earth shall awake, some to everlasting life and some to shame and everlasting contempt. And those who are wise shall shine like the brightness of the firmament; and those who turn many to righteousness, like the stars forever and ever. But you, Daniel, shut up the words, and seal the book, until the time of the end." (Daniel 12:1–4) This passage receives elaborate development in Revelation, the last book of the New Testament, with its details about the Book of Life and the seven seals that can be broken only by Christ, the Lamb who was slain.

As with Christianity, later Jewish thought reflects the influence of a Platonic belief in the immortality of the soul, but neither Christianity nor Judaism loses its grounding in a hope for the redemption of history. As many scholars have noted, the way that Jesus and the first Christians, who were all Jews, spoke about the resurrection of the dead assumed that the idea of such a resurrection was already well planted in Jewish piety. The body matters, as is evident in Jewish funeral practices. The body is not just the "mortal coil" that remains after the soul has taken its flight. Among observant Jews, there are strong inhibitions against both embalming and autopsy, and we have already discussed other customs of mourning and prayer that bind together the living and dead in powerful solidarity. This reflects the solidarity of body and soul, which, with the whole of reality encompassing us all, awaits a final redemption.

The sense of cosmic redemption does not detract from the undeniable specificity of a particular death. What Christians call "the last rites" for the dying have their counterpart in Jewish custom. The form is given in the *Shulhan Arukh*, a sixteenth-century code of law followed by observant Jews to this day. Usually, although not necessarily, a rabbi presides at this preparation for a good death.

> When one is approaching death, it is to be said to him [or her]: "Many have confessed and not died and many who did not confess did die. May it be that for the merit of confessing you will live. And all who do confess have a portion in the world-to-come." If he is unable to confess with his mouth, let him do it in his heart. And if he does not know the full confession, let him only say: "May my death be atonement for all my sins." . . . The form of confession is as follows: "I acknowledge before Thee Lord my God and God of my fathers that my healing and my death are in Thy hands. May it be Thy will that I be completely healed, but if I die, then let my death be atonement for all sins of carelessness, those done for pleasure, and those done in rebellion that I have sinned, transgressed, and rebelled against Thee. May my portion be in the Garden of Eden, and may I merit the world-to-come that is in store for the righteous." And if he wishes to confess at greater length, he may do so. (*Shulhan Arukh: Yoreh De'ah*, 338.1–2)

The idea that death is something that we owe may be deeply entrenched in the human consciousness. Sheridan wrote, "Death's a debt; his mandamus binds all alike—no bail no demurrer." As Shakespeare would have it in *Henry IV*, "A man can die but once; we owe God a death." In the Christian understanding, Christ died that we might live. And yet we die. We began this discussion of Judaism and Christianity by saying that death is not natural; it is not part of the way things were originally supposed to be. And yet it is undeniably part of the only human nature we are given to live. The idea that death is a debt to be paid by all the children of Adam and Eve, hints at some mysterious connection between death and redemption. The eternal pity is not untouched by purpose.

## 7.

A long time ago, when I was a young pastor in a very black and very poor inner-city parish that could not pay a salary, I worked part-time as chaplain at Kings County Hospital in Brooklyn. With more than three thousand beds, Kings County boasted then of being the largest medical center in the world. It seems primitive now, but thirty-five years ago not much of a fuss was made about those who were beyond reasonable hope of recovery. They were almost all poor people, and this was before Medicaid or Medicare, so it was, as we used to say, a charity hospital. They were sedated, and food was brought for those who could eat. The dying, male and female, had their beds lined up side by side in a huge ward, fifty to a hundred of them at any given time. On hot summer days and without air-conditioning, they would fitfully toss off sheets and undergarments. The scene of naked and half-naked bodies groaning and writhing was reminiscent of Dante's *Purgatorio*.

Hardly a twenty-four-hour stint would go by without my accompanying two or three or more people to their death. One such death is indelibly printed upon my memory. His name was Albert, a man of about seventy and (I don't know why it sticks in my mind) completely bald. That hot summer morning I had prayed with him and read the twenty-third Psalm. Toward evening, I went up again to the death ward—for so everybody called it—to see him again. Clearly the end was near. Although he had been given a sedative, he was entirely lucid. I put my left arm around his shoulder and together, face almost touching face, we prayed the Our Father. Then Albert's eyes opened wider, as though he had seen something in my expression. "Oh," he said, "Oh, don't be afraid." His body sagged back and he was dead. Stunned, I realized that, while I thought I was ministering to him, his last moment of life was expended in ministering to me.

There is another death that will not leave me. Charlie Williams was a deacon of St. John the Evangelist in Brooklyn. (We sometimes called the parish St. John the Mundane in order to distinguish it from St. John the Divine, the Episcopal cathedral up on Morningside Heights.) Charlie was an ever-ebullient and sustaining presence through rough times. In the face of every difficulty, he had no doubt but that "Jesus going to see us through." Then something went bad in his chest, and the doctors made medically erudite noises to cover their ignorance. I held his hand as he died a painful death at age forty-three. Through the blood that bubbled up from his hemorrhaging lungs he formed his last word—very quietly, not complaining but deeply puzzled, he looked up at me and said, "Why?"

Between Albert's calm assurance and Charlie's puzzlement, who is to say which is the Christian way to die? I have been with others who screamed defiance, and some who screamed with pain, and many who just went to sleep. Typically today the patient is heavily sedated and plugged into sundry machines. One only knows that death has come when the beeping lines on the monitors go flat or the attending physician nods his head in acknowledgment of medicine's defeat. It used to be that we accompanied sisters and brothers to their final encounter. Now we mostly sit by and wait. The last moment that we are really with them, and they with us, is in many cases hours or even many days before they die. But medical technology notwithstanding, for each one of them, for each one of us, at some point "it" happens. The Christian tradition has a great deal to say about "it." That teaching informs the ways in which Christians think about death and the evidence suggests that, at least in many cases, it forms the way they die.

**8.**

What the Christian tradition has to say about death is both straightforward and modest. It is straightforward in that it asserts that $X$ is to be said but $Y$ is not to be said. It is modest in that it acknowledges that everything that we say is necessarily inadequate. We are dealing with things that we cannot understand fully since they are beyond our experience. What we know from experience and what we can reasonably infer from what we know is joined to what is revealed by God. But God's revelation must be accommodated to our human understanding or else we would not understand it. Our human understanding, in turn, is limited and finite. And so Christians say with St. Paul, "Now I know in part; then I shall understand fully, even as I have been fully understood." (1 Corinthians 13:12)

Thus when it comes to death, as to so much else that transcends our understanding, we say it is a mystery. Some protest that saying something is a mystery is an evasion, even a cop-out. The response is that acknowledging both what we know and what we do not know is the course of unrelenting honesty. It is the alternative to the eating of the tree of knowledge of good and evil by which our first parents decided that they would determine what is true. The commonplace, indeed banal, expression of this primordial sin in our popular culture is that we decide what is true "for me."

In dealing with both the necessity and limitation of talking about things we cannot understand fully, Catholic Christians (but not only Catholics) typically speak of "analogy." An analogy is a comparison or similarity between things that are both like and unlike one another. For instance, "A is to B as C is to D." Theology is language about God, and all our language about God is analogous. That is because we can only compare God, the Creator, with the created things that we know. Thus every similarity between God and creatures (God is good; human beings are good) is understood to indicate a greater dissimilarity (God's goodness is unlike human goodness in that it infinitely surpasses it). The Fourth Lateran Council in 1215 put the matter succinctly: "No similarity can be found so great but that the dissimilarity is even greater." This may lead one to throw up one's hands in despair over ever saying anything for sure about a mystery. That would be the case were it not for the Christian confidence that experience can be trusted, reasoning on the basis of experience can be trusted, and, above all, revelation can be trusted. And all this is the case because God, who is Lord of all, can be trusted.

Analogical language, then, is more than just human speculation or groping after things that surpass our understanding. Christians believe that what their faith says about life and death—and about the One who is the source and end of all that is, ever was, and ever will be—is analogy that can be trusted and trusted absolutely. It can be trusted in the face of the mystery that is death. This brief discussion of analogy, of what we can know and what we cannot know, is simply to prepare the way for a short survey of what Christianity has to say about death. With Judaism—upon which Christianity is entirely dependent and without which it makes no sense at all—Christianity affirms that death is not "natural." It is not the way things were supposed to be in the beginning.

This is the way the *Catechism of the Catholic Church* puts it: "Scripture portrays the tragic consequences of this first disobedience. Adam and Eve immediately lose the grace of original holiness. They become afraid of the God of whom they have conceived a distorted image—that of a God jealous of his prerogatives. The harmony in which they had found themselves, thanks to original justice, is now destroyed: the control of the soul's spiritual faculties over the body is shattered; the union of man and woman becomes subject to tensions, their relations henceforth marked by lust and domination. Harmony with creation is broken: visible creation has become alien and hostile to man. Because of man, creation is now subject 'to its bondage to decay.' (Romans 8:21) Finally, the consequence explicitly foretold for this disobedience will come true: man will 'return to the ground' (Genesis 4:3–15), for out of it he was taken. *Death makes its entry into human history.*" (399, 400)

An awful lot is packed into that little paragraph. Note that the consequences of sin, including death, are precisely that: consequences, not punishments. Creating human beings with free will so that they could freely love him and one another—for love that is not free is not love at all—God "foretold" what would happen if they turned away from him. And, sure enough, that is what happened. The question inevitably arises: What would the world be like if there had been no sin and, therefore, no death? A thousand intellectual difficulties immediately propose themselves if we try to think of a world in which people lived forever. Never one to be intimidated by insuperable difficulties, the great St. Augustine (354–430) addresses the pertinent questions with considerable verve in Book XIII of his *City of God*. I will not go into the details here, but it makes for fascinating reading.

Suffice it that, had there been no sin and death, Christians would not hope for heaven, for heaven would be here on earth. Heaven is, quite simply, living in perfect fellowship with God who is everything good and true and beautiful, far beyond our capacity to imagine. Because sin and death did happen, the Christian hope is for a heaven that is the original state of the Garden of Eden restored, and then more. And then quite a bit more, actually. For one thing, since we will carry our personal identities with us, we will presumably have the memory of everything that has happened since that unfortunate afternoon in the garden. Another distinct improvement over the original state is that in heaven we will presumably not be able to fall into sin all over again, thus restarting the same dismal story of death's dominion.

But if in heaven we will not be able to sin, does that mean we will not have free will? And if we do not have free will, how will we be able to love freely? In response to such questions, please see above on "analogical language." Frankly, we are in over our heads here. The Christian view invites us to believe that our eternal destiny is not only an improvement over the original situation in the Garden of Eden, it is an infinite improvement. So much better is the prospect that in our contemplation of it we might even feel gratitude that our first parents fell into sin. In the great liturgy of the Easter Vigil, Christians call their fall a "happy fault" or, in the Latin, *felix culpa*. "O, happy fault that gave us such a great Redeemer!" the liturgy exults.

The prospect of a love that is absolutely and eternally secure is, of course, very different from our experience with the loves of this world. But then, so too is the idea of living forever and so much else in the Christian concept of heaven. The hope is for something genuinely new and unprecedented in our experience. "Then I saw a new heaven and a new earth," says the book of Revelation. "God will dwell with them, and they shall be his people . . . and he will wipe away every tear from their eyes, and death shall be no more, neither shall there be mourning nor crying nor pain any more, for the former things have passed away." (Revelation 21) All of this is quite candidly acknowledged to be beyond our comprehension. As St. Paul writes, echoing the Old Testament prophet Isaiah, "Eye has not seen, nor the ear heard, nor the heart conceived what God has prepared for those who love him." (1 Corinthians 2:9)

Earlier we mentioned those who suggest that the original fall into sin was really a "fall up" because it brought with it human consciousness as we know it. It is said that the life of primitive innocence is, well, so much less *interesting* than the conflicted life of our actual experience. So also there are those who think that heaven must be a very dull place. Unless one is crazy about music, who wants to be singing around the throne or playing harps forever and ever? And while it is very attractive to think there will be no more tears or mourning or crying or pain, aren't those things the necessary antitheses to joy, birth, laughter, and pleasure? Isn't there a necessary connection between the negative and the positive? In the world as we know it, the answer would seem to be yes. But not, or so Christians believe, in the new heaven and new earth.

In that happy circumstance, St Paul writes, "God will be all in all" (1 Corinthians 15:28), and one could only find that prospect dull if one thinks God is dull. In the Christian view that is unthinkable since, as the eleventh-century Anselm of Canterbury put it, "God is that than which nothing greater can be thought." God is always more. God is, so to speak, the nth degree of all that is true, good, and beautiful, and then more. It is this promise of perfect communion with the Absolute that transcends our present experience in which thesis is accompanied by antithesis, light by dark, joy by mourning, and life by death. The Christian understanding of death, then, is placed firmly within an understanding of all reality as centered in the life of God as reality's first cause and final end. In this context, St Paul, in the same passage, issues his defiant, almost taunting, challenge, "O death, where is thy victory? O grave, where is thy sting?"

For those sitting on the mourning bench of the eternal pity, however, that triumphant note will ring hollow if struck prematurely. We have already discussed the problem with upbeat funeral services that "celebrate life" in a way that short-circuits the *Dies Irae* of sin, loss, and judgment. A good many Christians, it must be admitted, have imbibed too well Platonic notions of an immortal soul floating off to paradise or even Buddhist ideas of the unreality of death, and therefore the unreality of life as well. The attitude seems to be, "Death? It's no big deal." But for those dying their own death and the death of those they love, death is a very big deal indeed. Don't tell them that it doesn't matter, that they'll get over it, that things will look brighter tomorrow. Death is, in the words of St Paul, "the last enemy." (1 Corinthians 15:26) The only consolation to be trusted is the consolation that is on the far side of the inconsolable.

Some Christian theologians, too, have followed philosophers who suggest that human life attains its fulfillment in death. But the mainstream of the Christian tradition has unblinkingly recognized that death does not fulfill life but terminates it. With the Jewish realism of the Old Testament, death is seen as separation from God in the realm of Sheol where no praise sounds. Yet our separation from God is not God's separation from us, for the power of Yhwh extends also to the kingdom of the dead. "Whither shall I go from thy Spirit? Or whither shall I flee from thy presence? If I ascend to heaven, thou art there! If I make my bed in Sheol, thou art there!" (Psalm 139:7–8).

Where God is, there is life. We ask, Why is there death? We might better ask, Why is there life? The biblical view is that life is created by the divine spirit. If life comes from God, then death, which is separation from life, is separation from God. This is the essential connection between sin and death. Sin is turning away from God, who is the source of life, and therefore death inevitably follows.

This view would seem to be very different from, even incompatible with, modern biology's claim that life is a function of the living cell. But maybe not. The Protestant theologian, Paul Tillich, wrote that the heart of being in sin is that "man is outside the divine center to which his own center essentially belongs." The sinner has become "the center of himself and of his world." This is the pride or hubris that makes us want to be our own god. St Augustine's term for such hubris is *amor sui,* the love of self. When we make ourselves the center of our own world, we become radically disconnected from the very center of our being, and the result is dis-integration. Sickness is a disintegration of the organism's centeredness; the organism goes off on its own. In a cancer, for instance, an organism may be strong and healthy and growing. The potentially fatal problem is that it is a disordered strength, a de-centered healthiness, and a growth that has no regard for the body of which it is part.

In a very important respect, cancer is not so much a sickness as a form of rambunctious healthiness that has broken away from its orientation toward the source and end of life. This is graphically described by Dr. Sherwin Nuland in his book, *How We Die:*

> Cancer, far from being a clandestine foe, is in fact berserk with the malicious exuberance of killing. The disease pursues a continuous, uninhibited, circumferential, barn-burning expedition of destructiveness, in which it heeds no rules, follows no commands, and explodes all resistance in a homicidal riot of devastation. Its cells behave like the members of a barbarian horde run amok—leaderless and undirected, but with a single-minded purpose: to plunder everything within reach. This is what medical scientists mean when they use the word *autonomy.* The form and rate of multiplication of the murderous cells violate every rule of decorum within the living animal whose vital nutrients nourish it only to be destroyed by this enlarging atrocity that has sprung newborn from its own protoplasm. In this sense, cancer is not a parasite. Galen was wrong to call it *praeter naturam,* "outside of nature." Its first cells are the bastard offspring of unsuspecting parents who

ultimately reject them because they are ugly, deformed, and unruly. In the community of living tissues, the uncontrolled mob of misfits that is cancer behaves like a gang of perpetually wilding adolescents. They are the juvenile delinquents of cellular society.

Sin is the declaration of *autonomy* from the source of life, and thus the consequence of sin is the opposite of life, which is death. Originally and persistently, sin is wanting to know and decide good and evil for ourselves, rather than depending on God's definition of good and evil. The "essence" of illness, writes the medical philosopher V. von Weiszacker, is "in a kind of estrangement from oneself." "The common factor in all illnesses is therefore to be found in a departure from the right order of life." With the entrance of sin, the world— both spiritual and physical—went wildly out of whack. This Christian concept takes very seriously both body and soul. There is, of course, a difference between physical and spiritual death. Augustine wrote that physical death is the separation of the soul from the body, while spiritual death is the separation of the soul from God. But the Christian concern is for both the spiritual and the physical.

Just as the hope is for a new heaven *and a new earth,* so the basic Christian creeds anticipate "the resurrection of the body." The final redemption must encompass the whole of creation, including the physical. The resurrection of the body is central in Canto Fourteen of Dante's *Paradiso:*

> When glorified and sanctified, the flesh
> is once again our dress, our persons shall
> in being all complete, please all the more;
> therefore, whatever light gratuitous
> the Highest Good gives us will be *enhanced*—
> the light that will allow us to see Him
> that light will cause our vision to increase.

The *visio Dei,* the vision of God, is the fulfillment toward which all human life is innerly directed. That vision will be more radiant, it will be "enhanced," when the soul is rejoined with the flesh "now covered by the earth." As coals burn with a more intense glow than an immaterial flame, so also our bodies will bring to perfection our vision of God. This concept is in sharp contrast to the Platonic idea that the soul reaches perfection after it is rid of the unworthy encumbrance of the body.

All kinds of questions immediately arise. Will we have in eternity the *same* body we had on earth? Will it bear the scars and ravages of its earthly sojourn? How old will the resurrected body be? Obviously, such questions occurred also to St. Paul, who writes at the conclusion of 1 Corinthians: "With what kind of body do they come? What you sow is not the body that is to be but a bare kernel, perhaps of wheat or some other grain. But God gives it a body as he has chosen, and to each kind of seed its own body. . . . It is sown a physical body, it is raised a spiritual body."

The term "spiritual body" may seem like an oxymoron. After all, we might think, the physical is physical and the spiritual is spiritual. But recall again the Old Testament understanding of the spirit of Yhwh as the source of life, and we can perhaps begin to understand the concept of the whole creation newly recharged with the spirit of the living God. Yet there is no doubt that, with St. Paul, we reach the limits of human language and comprehension in trying to envision the new heaven and new earth. The irrepressible conviction is that the body is part of the *self*, and without the body the self is not whole. "In my flesh I shall see God," the suffering Job cried out (19:26), and so the Christian tradition continues to echo that cry.

For Christians, of course, this confident cry turns most crucially upon the bodily resurrection of Jesus, who is, as the New Testament declares, "the first fruits" of the new creation. After the resurrection, his body was different. He seemed to pass through walls (John 20:26), and his disciples did not at first recognize the resurrected Jesus (Luke 24:16). The Christian claim is that we will be "like him," without presuming to explain precisely what that means. The hope is not contingent upon our understanding the precise shape of what we hope for. Paul again: "If there is no resurrection of the dead, then Christ has not been raised; if Christ has not been raised, then our preaching is in vain and your faith is in vain. . . . If for this life only we have hoped in Christ, we are of all men most to be pitied." (1 Corinthians 15:13 f.)

Finally, analysis gives way to doxology and explanation dissolves into praise:

> Lo! I tell you a mystery. We shall not all sleep, but we shall all be changed, in a moment, in the twinkling of an eye, at the last trumpet. For the trumpet will sound, and the dead will be raised imperishable, and we shall be changed. For this perishable nature must put on the imperishable, and this mortal nature must put on immortality. When the perishable puts on the imperishable, and the mortal puts on immortality, then shall come to pass the saying that is written: 'Death is swallowed up in victory.' 'O death, where is thy victory? O grave, where is thy sting?' (1 Corinthians 15:51 f.)

The completion for which we yearn would not be complete without our bodies. Again Dante: "One and the other choir seemed to me / so quick and keen to say 'Amen' that they / showed clearly how they longed for their dead bodies." For the thirteenth-century German mystic, Mechthild of Magdenburg, the body is the way of knowing God. Though her body was the source of pain, she could not bear the thought of being separated from it. "The love of God lies on me. And when I think that my body will be lost in death and I shall no longer be able to suffer for Jesus or to praise him, this is so heavy to me that I long, if it were possible, to live until Judgment Day. My love forces me to this."

The modern notion of the psychosomatic unity of the human being—the unity of body, mind, and spirit—has deep roots in Judaism and Christianity. In her wonderful study, *The Resurrection of the Body in Western Christianity,* Caroline Bynum acknowledges the philosophical difficulties raised by the resurrection of the body, but she concludes: "For however absurd it seems—and some of the greatest theologians have grappled with that absurdity—it is a concept of sublime courage and optimism. It locates redemption where ultimate horror also resides—in pain, mutilation, death, and decay. . . . It was the stench and fragmentation they saw lifted to glory in resurrection."

God is infinite, we human beings are finite. In our existence in time, finitude necessarily entails death. But, Christians believe, it will not be so in "the eternal present" of perfect communion with God. We will still be finite, but we will not die. What we call death is, for the believer, entrance into the fullness of the life of God that is lived by the resurrected Jesus—a life in which Christians participate already now. In this light, some noted Christian thinkers have actually called death a good thing. The contemporary historian, Jaroslav Pelikan, goes so far as to speak of "the gospel of death." Comparing the Christian understanding with the views of Eastern religions, he writes: "Although the idea of cycles promises immortality beyond the arc of this bounded existence, it actually holds out the prospect of an endless karma from which even the merciful forgetfulness of death is no escape. In antithesis to this, the Christian gospel of death announces to men the gracious message that they will die once and for all." One must keep in mind, however, that this apparent insouciance about death is always and entirely premised upon an event that is on the far side of death, namely, the resurrection of Jesus.

In discussing the second-century church father, Irenaeus, Pelikan writes:

Having taken on flesh, Christ is obedient to the death of the cross. To live a genuine human life means to live a life that is formed by the shape of death. By going through death rather than around death, he transforms the shape of death into the shape of life. . . . This is what makes the coming of Christ literally a matter of life and death. His history must be as genuine a part of the human story as the history of Adam or the history of any other man. Irenaeus defends the genuineness

of this history with all the passion and rhetoric he can summon against the heretics who transform the story of Christ into something less than history in their
effort to transform it into something more than history. Only if his history is a
real history can it save men who live and die in real history.

At the end of the twentieth century, as in the second century, there are
many Christians (it is not polite to call them "heretics" today) who "transform
the story of Christ into something less than history in their effort to transform
it into something more than history." Both Judaism and Christianity are ada-
mant in their insistence that what we experience as real is really real. As Caroline
Bynum says, the only redemption worthy of our hope is a redemption located
"where ultimate horror also resides—in pain, mutilation, death, and decay."
The only answer that rings true is the answer that is on the far side of having
plumbed the deepest depths of the eternal pity. And that is why what Christianity has to say about death and life is centered in a sign of dereliction, the
God-Man hanging on a cross.

### 9.

The readings collected here are by believers and agnostics of various kinds.
The selections are not all of the genre generally described as "edifying." Far
from it. Some believers rail against death, and others confess no faith but en-
trust themselves to what must be. Tolstoy's Ivan Ilych cannot die until he is
forced to acknowledge that he has not really lived, and then "there was no fear
because there was no death." C. S. Lewis, the noted Christian apologist, demands of himself an unflinching experience of death's robbery for which there
is no compensation, while Jeffrey Ford provides the view that death is an unnecessary unpleasantness to be evaded by mercy killing. Peter De Vries throws
his outrage at a crucified Christ who, we are left to infer, extends his arms to
be hit again. Christian de Chergé's "Last Testament" testifies to a sighting of
the face of God in the face of the terrorist who kills him, leaving us to wonder
whether human beings are really capable of such love, and hoping that they
are—hoping that we are.

For all of us, the time will come. That is the most banal and unsettling of
observations. On January 8, 1997, the Supreme Court held oral argument on
circuit court rulings supporting doctor-assisted suicide. Several justices were
troubled by the claim that assisted killing could be limited to those who are
near death. A lawyer in favor of the proposed measures explained that the difference is that for such people "the dying process has already begun." Justice
Antonin Scalia responded, "I hate to tell you, but the dying process has already

begun for all of us." That is the case for the young who deny it and for the not-so-young who must work hard to deny it. The view is urged that we have to die and get out of the way in order to make room for those who come after us. Tennyson wrote, "Old men must die; or the world would grow moldy, would only breed the past again." We may know the wish is ignoble and yet wish that an exception might be made for ourselves. But for all the vaunted advances in medical technology, the mortality rate, as mentioned earlier, continues to be one hundred percent.

It has often been said that each death is unique, that each of us must die our own death. Enthusiasts such as Walt Whitman gild the inevitable. "Nothing can happen more beautiful than death," he wrote in *Leaves of Grass*. In *Song of Myself* he trumpets: "Has anyone supposed it lucky to be born? / I hasten to inform him or her, it is just as lucky to die, and I know it." Good for him. "Why fear death?" asked Charles Frohman as he went down with the sinking *Lusitania*. "Death is only a beautiful adventure." Fare thee well, Mr. Frohman. If each life is unique, and it is, then it would seem to follow that each death is unique. I will not dispute the logic of that. And there is no doubt an element of adventure in moving into the unknown. But in my own experience of dying, it struck me as so very commonplace, even trite, that this life should end this way. Perhaps I should explain.

### 10.

Several lawyers have told me that it would make a terrific malpractice suit. All I would have to do is make a deposition and then answer a few questions in court, if it ever came to trial, which it probably wouldn't since the insurance companies would be eager to settle. It would be, I was assured, a very big settlement. The statute of limitations has not run out as of this writing. But I will not sue, mainly because it would somehow sully my gratitude for being returned from the jaws of death. Gratitude is too precious and too fragile to keep company with what looks suspiciously like revenge.

The stomach pains and intestinal cramps had been coming on for almost a year. My regular physician, a Park Avenue doctor of excellent reputation, had told me long ago how pleased he was with the new techniques for colonoscopy. It meant, he said, that none of his patients need die of colon cancer. His partner, the specialist in these matters, did one colonoscopy and, some weeks later, another. After each mildly painful probing up through the intestines, he was glad to tell me that there was nothing there. Then, on Sunday afternoon, January 10, 1993, about five o'clock, after four days of intense discomfort in which there was yet another probe and yet another X-ray, I was at home suddenly doubled over on the floor with nausea and pain. The sensation was of my stomach exploding.

A friend who was visiting phoned the doctor's office, but he was on vacation. The physician covering for him listened to the symptoms and prescribed a powerful laxative. (I said that this story would smack of the commonplace.) Much later, other doctors said that the prescription might, more than possibly, have been fatal. They said they never heard of several colonoscopies not detecting a tumor, and shook their heads over a physician who would prescribe a laxative after being apprised of symptoms indicating something much more serious was wrong.

The friend had the presence of mind to bundle me off—pushing, pulling, half-carrying me—to the nearest emergency room, which, fortunately, was only a block from the house. The place was crowded. I strongly recommend always having with you an aggressive friend or two when you go to a hospital and are really sick. A large and imperiously indifferent woman at the desk was not about to let anyone jump the line of waiting cases, relenting only when the friend gave signs that he was not averse to the use of physical violence. She then sat me down to answer a long list of questions about symptoms and medical insurance, which I tried to answer until I fell off the chair in a faint, at which point she surmised she had an emergency on her hands. The experience so far did not instill confidence in the care I was likely to receive.

Very soon, however, I was flat on my back on a gurney, surrounded by tubes, machines, and technicians exhibiting their practiced display of frenetic precision, just like on television. The hospital's chief surgeon, who happened to be on duty that night, ordered an X-ray that showed a large tumor in the colon and declared there was no time to lose. I was wheeled at great speed down the halls for an elevator to the operating room, only to discover the elevators were out of order. By then I had been sedated and was feeling no pain. In fact, I was somewhat giddy and recall trying to make a joke about the contrast between the high-tech medicine and the broken-down elevators. A guard showed up who said he knew how to get number six elevator working, and then I was looking up at the white water-stained ceiling of the operating room, and then there was someone putting a mask over my face and telling me to breathe deeply, and then there was "Now I lay me down to sleep . . . ," and then there was the next morning.

The operation took several hours and was an unspeakable mess. The tumor had expanded to rupture the intestine; blood, fecal matter, and guts all over the place. My stomach was sliced open from the rib case down to the pubic area, then another slice five inches to the left from the navel for a temporary colostomy. I've noticed that in such cases the doctors always seem to say that the tumor was "as big as a grapefruit," but my surgeon insists the blackish gray glob was the size of "a big apple." After they had sewed me up, the hemorrhaging began, they knew not from where. Blood pressure collapsed and other vital signs began to fade. What to do? The surgeon advised my friend to call the immediate family and let them know I would likely not make it through the night. The doctors debated. To open me up all over again might kill me. On the other hand, if they didn't find and stop the hemorrhaging I was surely dead.

Of course they went in again. The source of the effusion of blood was the spleen, "nicked," as the surgeon said, in the ghastliness of the first surgery. Given the circumstances, I'm surprised that parts more vital were not nicked. The spleen removed and the blood flow stanched, they sewed me up again and waited to see if I would live. The particulars of that night, of course, I was told after the event. "It was an interesting case," one doctor opined in a friendly manner. "It was as though you had been hit twice by a Mack truck going sixty miles an hour. I didn't think you'd survive."

My first clear memory is of the next morning, I don't know what time. I am surrounded by doctors and technicians talking in a worried tone about why I am not coming to. I heard everything that was said and desperately wanted to respond, but I was locked into absolute immobility, incapable of moving an eyelash or twitching a toe. The sensation was that of being encased in marble; pink marble, I thought, such as is used for gravestones. The surgeon repeatedly urged me to move my thumb, but it was impossible. Then I heard, "The Cardinal is here." It was my bishop, John Cardinal O'Connor. He spoke directly into my right ear, repeatedly calling my name. Then, "Richard, wriggle your nose." It was a plea and a command, and I wanted to do it more urgently than anything I have ever wanted to do in my life. The trying, the sheer exercise of will to wriggle my nose, seemed to go on and on, and then I felt a twinge, no more than a fraction of a millimeter, and the Cardinal said, "He did it! He did it!" "I didn't see anything," said the surgeon. So I tried again, and I did it again, and everybody saw it, and the Cardinal and the doctors and the technicians all began to exclaim what a wonderful thing it was, as though one had risen from the dead.

The days in the intensive care unit were an experience familiar to anyone who has ever been there. I had never been there before, except to visit others, and that is nothing like being there. I was struck by my disposition of utter passivity. There was absolutely nothing I could do or wanted to do, except to lie there and let them do whatever they do in such a place. Indifferent to time, I neither knew nor cared whether it was night or day. I recall counting sixteen different tubes and other things plugged into my body before I stopped counting. From time to time, it seemed several times an hour but surely could not have been, a strange young woman with a brown wool hat and heavy gold necklace would come by and whisper, "I want blood." She stuck in a needle and took blood, smiling mysteriously all the time. She could have said she wanted to cut off my right leg and I would probably have raised no objection. So busy was I with just being there, with one thought that was my one and every thought: "I almost died."

Astonishment and passivity were strangely mixed. I confess to having thought of myself as a person very much in charge. Friends, meaning, I am sure, no unkindness, had sometimes described me as a control freak. Now there was nothing to be done, nothing that I could do, except be there. Here comes a most curious part of the story, and readers may make of it what they will. In the readings gathered here, Carol Zaleski provides an insightful reflection on "near death" experiences. I had always been skeptical of such tales. I am much less so now. I am inclined to think of it as a "near life" experience, and it happened this way.

It was a couple of days after leaving intensive care, and it was night. I could hear patients in adjoining rooms moaning and mumbling and occasionally calling out; the surrounding medical machines were pumping and sucking and bleeping as usual. Then, all of a sudden, I was jerked into an utterly lucid state of awareness. I was sitting up in the bed staring intently into the darkness, although in fact I knew my body was lying flat. What I was staring at was a color like blue and purple, and vaguely in the form of hanging drapery. By the drapery were two "presences." I saw them and yet did not see them, and I cannot explain that. But they were there, and I knew that I was not tied to the bed. I was able and prepared to get up and go somewhere. And then the presences—one or both of them, I do not know—spoke. This I heard clearly. Not in an ordinary way, for I cannot remember anything about the voice. But the message was beyond mistaking: "Everything is ready now."

That was it. They waited for a while, maybe for a minute. Whether they were waiting for a response or just waiting to see whether I had received the message, I don't know. "Everything is ready now." It was not in the form of a command, nor was it an invitation to do anything. They were just letting me know. Then they were gone, and I was again flat on my back with my mind racing wildly. I had an iron resolve to determine right then and there what had happened. Had I been dreaming? In no way. I was then and was now as lucid and wide awake as I had ever been in my life.

Tell me that I was dreaming and you might as well tell me that I am dreaming that I wrote the sentence before this one. Testing my awareness, I pinched myself hard, and ran through the multiplication tables, and recalled the birth dates of my seven brothers and sisters, and my wits were vibrantly about me. The whole thing had lasted three or four minutes, maybe less. I resolved at that moment that I would never, never let anything dissuade me from the reality of what had happened. Knowing myself, I expected I would later be inclined to doubt it. It was an experience as real, as powerfully confirmed by the senses, as anything I have ever known. That was almost seven years ago. Since then I have not had a moment in which I was seriously tempted to think it did not happen. It happened—as surely, as simply, as undeniably as it happened that I tied my shoelaces this morning. I could as well deny the one as deny the other, and were I to deny either I would surely be mad.

"Everything is ready now." I would be thinking about that incessantly during the months of convalescence. My theological mind would immediately go to work on it. They were angels, of course. *Angelos* simply means "messenger." There were no white robes or wings or anything of that sort. As I said, I did not see them in any ordinary sense of the word. But there was a message; therefore there were messengers. Clearly, the message was that I could go somewhere with them. Not that I must go or should go, but simply that they were ready if I was. Go where? To God, or so it seemed. I understood that they were ready to get me ready to see God. It was obvious enough to me that I was not prepared, in my present physical and spiritual condition, for the beatific vision, for seeing God face to face. They were ready to get me ready. This comports with the doctrine of purgatory, that there is a process of purging and preparation to get us ready to meet God. I should say that their presence was entirely friendly. There was nothing sweet or cloying, and there was no urgency about it. It was as though they just wanted to let me know. The decision was mine as to when or whether I would take them up on the offer.

There is this about being really sick, you get an enormous amount of attention. I cannot say that I did not enjoy it. In the pain and the nausea and the boredom without end, there were times when I was content to lie back and enjoy the attention. It was a kind of compensation. Over these days there were hundreds of cards and letters and phone calls and, later, brief visits—the last by people who sometimes betrayed the hope of having a final word with what they took to be their dying friend. Some of those who checked in I had not seen in years. Nor have I seen them since, so busy are we with our several busynesses. Sickness is an enforced pause for the counting up of our friends, and being grateful.

In all the cards and letters assuring me of prayer, and almost all did offer such assurance, there were notable differences. Catholics say they are "storming the gates of heaven" on your behalf, and have arranged to have masses said. Evangelical Protestants are "lifting you up before the throne." Mainline Protestants, Jews, and the unaffiliated let it go with a simple "I am praying for you," or "You are in my prayers." One gets the impression that Catholics and evangelicals are more aggressive on the prayer front.

Then there were longer letters laying out the case for my getting better. A friend who is a constitutional scholar at an ivy league university wrote a virtual lawyer's brief summing up the reasons for dying and the reasons for living, and came down strongly on the side of my living. It was very odd, because after that there were a number of similar letters, all arguing that I should stay around for a while and assuming that I was undecided about that. I was undecided. This struck me as strange: At the time of crisis and in the months of recovery following, I was never once afraid. I don't claim it as a virtue; it was simply the fact. It had less to do with courage than with indifference. Maybe this is "holy indifference," what the spiritual manuals describe as "a quality in a person's love for God above all that excludes preferences for any person, object, or condition of life." Aquinas, St. John of the Cross, and Ignatius Loyola all write at length about such holy indifference. All I know is that I was surprisingly indifferent to whether I would live or die. It probably had less to do with holiness than with my knowing that there was nothing I could do about it one way or another.

On the other hand, there was the message: "Everything is ready now." As though the decision were mine, to stay or to go. A friend who had written with his son the story of his son's several years of waging a heroic battle against a horrific series of cancers sent me their book, inscribed with the admonition "to fight relentlessly for life." It was very kind, but I was not at all disposed to fight. More to the point were those letters calmly laying out the reasons why it would be better for others, if not for me, were I to live rather than to die. Over the slow weeks and slower months of recovery, I gradually came to agree. But still very tentatively.

When I was recuperating at home and could take phone calls, those calls became a staple of everyday existence. There were dozens of calls daily; closer friends called every day. Somebody was always on call waiting. I enjoyed it shamelessly. Although I was often too tired to talk, when I had the energy I related in detail, over and over again, every minuscule change in my condition. With a credible display of intense interest, people listened to the problems with colostomy bags and the latest wrinkle in controlling the nausea that came with chemotherapy. And always in my talking, I was on the edge of tears. I, who had seldom cried in my adult life, was regularly, and without embarrassment, blubbering. Not in sadness. Not at all. But in a kind of amazement that this had happened to me, and maybe I was going to die and maybe I was going to live, and it was all quite out of my control. That was it, I think: I was not in charge, and it was both strange and very good not to be in charge.

Tentatively, I say, I began to think that I might live. It was not a particularly joyful prospect. Everything was shrouded by the thought of death, that I had almost died, that I may still die, that everyone and everything is dying. As much as I was grateful for all the calls and letters, I harbored a secret resentment. These friends who said they were thinking about me and praying for me all the time, I knew they also went shopping and visited their children and tended to their businesses, and there were long times when they were not thinking about me at all. More important, they were forgetting the primordial, overwhelming, indomitable fact: We are dying! Why weren't they as crushingly impressed by that fact as I was?

After a month or so, I could, with assistance, walk around the block. Shuffle is the more accurate term; irrationally fearing with every step that my stomach would rip open again. I have lived in New York almost forty years and have always been a fierce chauvinist about the place. When you're tired of London, you're tired of life, said the great Dr. Johnson. I had always thought that about New York, where there is more terror and tenderness per square foot than any place in the world. I embraced all the clichés about the place—the palpable vitality of its streets, the electricity in the air, and so forth and so on. Shuffling around the block and then, later, around several blocks, I was tired of it. Death was everywhere. The children at the playground at 19th Street and Second Avenue I saw as corpses covered with putrefying skin. The bright young model prancing up Park Avenue with her portfolio under her arm and dreaming of the success she is to be, doesn't she know she's going to die, that she's already dying? I wanted to cry out to everybody and everything, "Don't you know what's happening?" But I didn't. Let them be in their innocence and ignorance. It didn't matter. Nothing mattered.

Surprising to me, and to others, I did what had to be done with my work. I read manuscripts, wrote my columns, made editorial decisions, but all listlessly. It didn't really matter. After some time, I could shuffle the few blocks to the church and say Mass. At the altar, I cried a lot, and hoped the people didn't notice. To think that I'm really here after all, I thought, at the altar, at the *axis mundi*, the center of life. And of death. I would be helped back to the house, and days beyond numbering I would simply lie on the sofa looking out at the back yard. That birch tree, which every winter looked as dead as dead could be, was budding again. Would I be here to see it in full leaf, to see its leaves fall in the autumn? Never mind. It doesn't matter.

When I was a young man a parishioner told me, "Do all your praying before you get really sick. When you're sick you can't really pray." She was right, at least in largest part. Being really sick—vomiting, and worrying about what will show up on the next blood test, and trying to ignore the pain at three o'clock in the morning—is a full-time job. At best, you want to recede into relatively painless passivity, and listen to your older sister reading Willa Cather, as my sister read to me. During those long nights, *My Antonia, Death*

*Comes for the Archbishop, Shadows on the Rock,* and at those times I could have wished it to go on and on. Not that it mattered, but it was ever so pleasant being ever so pampered.

People are different around the very sick, especially when they think they may be dying. In the hospital, bishops came to visit and knelt by my bedside, asking for a blessing. A Jewish doctor, professing himself an atheist, asked for my prayers with embarrassed urgency. His wife had cancer, he explained, "And you know about that now." Call it primitive instinct or spiritual insight, but there is an aura about the sick and dying. They have crossed a line into a precinct others do not know. It is the aura of redemptive suffering, of suffering "offered up" on behalf of others, because there is nothing else to be done with it and you have to do something with it. The point is obvious but it impressed me nonetheless: When you are really sick it is impossible to imagine what it is like to be really well; and when you are well it is almost impossible to remember what it was like to be really sick. They are different precincts.

I had lost nearly fifty pounds and was greatly weakened. There was still another major surgery to come, to reverse the colostomy. You don't want to know the messy details. It was not the most dangerous surgery, but it was the third Mack truck, and for a long time afterward I barely had strength to lift my hand. Then, step by almost imperceptible step, I was recovering and dared to hope that I would be well again, that I would stride down the street again, that I would take on new projects again. Very little things stand out like luminous signposts. The first time I was able to take a shower by myself. It was dying and rising again in baptismal flood. When I was sent home from the hospital and told that, if I did not urinate by five o'clock, I should come back to the emergency room and someone would put the catheter back in, my heart sank. It was quite irrational, but going back to the emergency room would have been like recapitulating the entire ordeal of these last several months. I could not endure the thought. When at four o'clock I peed a strong triumphant pee, my heart was lifted on high, and with tears of gratitude I began to sing with feeble voice a Te Deum. I thought, "I am going to get better." And I allowed myself, ever so tentatively, to be glad.

That was almost seven years ago. I feel very well now. They tell me I might be around for another twenty years or so. The doctors say, perhaps somewhat arbitrarily, that five years marks complete recovery when you are restored to your age slot on the actuarial charts. The tests continue. Next Monday we get the latest report on the CEA (Carcinoembryonic Antigen), the blood indicator of cancerous activity, although my doctor says the test is not really necessary. I think I am well now. It took a long time after the surgeries, almost two years, before the day came when I suddenly realized that the controlling thought that day had not been the thought of death. And now, in writing this little essay, it all comes back. I remember where I have been, and where I will be again, and where we will all be.

There is nothing that remarkable in my story, except that we are all unique in our living and dying. The stories, poems, and reflections in the following pages speak of the eternal pity in other and, I expect, more compelling ways. Early on in my illness a friend gave me John Donne's wondrous *Devotions Upon Emergent Occasions,* and there is here an excerpt from that, including his well-known "No man is an island." The *Devotions* were written a year after Donne had almost died, and then lingered for months by death's door. He writes, "Though I may have seniors, others may be elder than I, yet I have proceeded apace in a good university, and gone a great way in a little time, by the furtherance of a vehement fever." So I too have been to a good university, and what I have learned, what I have learned most importantly, is that, in living and in dying, everything is ready now.

Part I

# THINKING ABOUT DYING:
# TWELVE CLASSIC VISIONS

# 1. THE CERTAINTY OF DEATH

*A thousand poetic commonplaces all declare the same thing—that living can only end in dying; that every step we take brings us closer to the grave. The English poet George Herbert (1593–1633) often turns to death in his poems, seeking some new expression of the fact that all that lives must die. In "Mortification," he traces with simple and homely images five stages in life—and, deliberately turning each image into a figure for dying, produces some of the most brutal lines ever written about the certainty of death. A baby's swaddling becomes a shroud, a boy's bed a grave, a youth's music a funeral bell, a man's home a coffin, and an old man's chair a bier. Rhyming "breath" with "death" in every stanza, Herbert insists on the equation of living with dying: Simply by being alive, we rehearse our funerals. And yet, just as he turns images of life to death in the first five stanzas, so he marvelously returns his images of death back to life in the sudden prayer of the poem's final two lines. If we understand that what seems to us living is actually dying, we may at last be ready to understand that what seems to us dying is actually living.*

# George Herbert, "Mortification"

How soon doth man decay!
When clothes are taken from a chest of sweets
To swaddle infants, whose young breath
Scarce knows the way,
Those clouts are little winding sheets,
Which do consign and send them unto death.

When boys go first to bed,
They step into their voluntary graves,
Sleep binds them fast; only their breath
Makes them not dead:
Successive nights, like rolling waves,
Convey them quickly, who are bound for death.

When youth is frank and free,
And calls for music, while his veins do swell,
All day exchanging mirth and breath
In company;
That music summons to the knell,
Which shall befriend him at the hour of death.

When man grows staid and wise,
Getting a house and home, where he may move
Within the circle of his breath,
Schooling his eyes;
That dumb enclosure maketh love
Unto the coffin, that attends his death.

When age grows low and weak,
Marking his grave, and thawing ev'ry year;
Till all do melt, and drown his breath
When he would speak;
A chair or litter shows the bier,
Which shall convey him to the house of death.

Man, 'ere he is aware,
Hath put together a solemnity
And dressed his hearse, while he has breath
As yet to spare:
Yet Lord, instruct us so to die,
That all these dyings may be life in death.

# 2. THE FIGURE OF DEATH

*From ancient sculpture to medieval pictures of the "Dance of Death," nearly every culture has made a personified figure of Death. In this Hindu selection, Death appears more lively than he is usually portrayed. A man named Wajashrawas once sacrificed to the gods all that he owned—until at last, angry at his son's questioning, he vowed to sacrifice even his son Nachiketas. But when Nachiketas, granted the death-boon of answered questions, asked Death what happens when we die, Death became almost human: begging to be released from replying, and then, forced to answer, expounding at last the doctrine of* brahman, *the universal soul, and its identity with the* at-man, *the individual soul. After death, some are reborn as humans, some as higher or lower things, but only those who discover that all souls are one escape the cycle of death and reincarnation. Composed in India in the tenth century* B.C., *the Upanishads are the speculative and mystical writings that form the final sections of the sacred scriptures of Hinduism. Of the 112 Upanishads, the* Katha-Upanishad *remains the best known in the West.*

# The *Katha-Upanishad*

Wajashrawas, wanting heaven, gave away all his property.

He had a son named Nachiketas. While the gifts were being given away, Nachiketas . . . went to his father and said, "Father, have you given me to somebody?" He repeated the question a second and a third time; at last his father said, "I give you to Death." . . . Wajashrawas would have taken back his words but Nachiketas said, "Think of those who went before, those that will come after: their word their bond. Man dies and is born again like a blade of grass."

Nachiketas went into the forest and sat in meditation within the house of Death. When Death appeared . . . , he said to Nachiketas, "A guest should be respected; you have lived three days in my house without eating and drinking. I bow to you, holy man! Take from me three gifts. . . . "

Nachiketas said, "Some say that when man dies he continues to exist, others that he does not. Explain, and that shall be my third gift."

Death said, "This question has been discussed by the gods, it is deep and difficult. Choose another gift, Nachiketas! Do not be hard. Do not compel me to explain."

Nachiketas said, "Death! you say that the gods have discussed it, that it is deep and difficult; what explanation can be as good as yours? What gift compares with that?"

Death said, "Take sons and grandsons, all long-lived, cattle and horses, elephants and gold, take a great kingdom. Anything but this—wealth, long life, Nachiketas! empire, anything whatever; satisfy the heart's desire. Pleasures beyond human reach, fine women with carriages, their musical instruments; mount beyond dreams; enjoy. But do not ask what lies beyond death."

Nachiketas said, "Destroyer of man! these things pass. Joy ends enjoyment, the longest life is short. Keep those horses, keep singing and dancing, keep it all for yourself. Wealth cannot satisfy a man. If he but please you, Master of All, he can live as long as he likes, get all that he likes; but I will not change my gift. What man, subject to death and decay, getting the chance of undecaying life, would still enjoy mere long life, thinking of copulation and beauty. Say where man goes after death; end all that discussion. This, which you have made so mysterious, is the only gift I will take."

Death said, "The good is one, the pleasant another; both command the soul. Who follows the good, attains sanctity; who follows the pleasant, drops out of the race. Every man faces both. The mind of the wise man draws him to the good, the flesh of the fool drives him to the pleasant.

"Nachiketas! Having examined the pleasures, you have rejected them; turned from the vortex of life and death. Diverging roads: one called ignorance, the other wisdom. Rejecting images of pleasure, Nachiketas! you turn towards wisdom. Fools brag of their knowledge; proud, ignorant, dissolving, blind led by the blind, staggering to and fro. What can the money-maddened simpleton know of the future? 'This is the only world,' cries he; because he thinks there is no other, I kill him again and again. . . . The wise, meditating on God, concentrating their thought, discovering in the mouth of the cavern, deeper in the cavern, that Self, that ancient Self, difficult to imagine, more difficult to understand, pass beyond joy and sorrow." . . .

Nachiketas asked, "What lies beyond right and wrong, beyond cause and effect, beyond past and future?"

Death said, " . . . The Self knows all, is not born, does not die, is not the effect of any cause, is eternal, self-existent, imperishable, ancient. How can the killing of the body kill Him? He who thinks that he kills, he who thinks that he is killed is ignorant. He does not kill nor is he killed. The Self is lesser than the least, greater than the greatest. He lives in all hearts. When senses are at rest, free from desire, man finds Him and mounts beyond sorrow. Though sitting, he travels; though sleeping is everywhere. Who but Death can understand that God is beyond joy and sorrow? Who knows the Self, bodiless among the embodied, unchanging among the changing, prevalent everywhere, goes beyond sorrow? . . . The wicked man is restless, without concentration, without peace; how can he find Him, whatever his learning? He has made mere preachers and soldiers His food, death its condiment; how can a common man find Him? Get up! Stir yourself! Learn wisdom at the Master's feet. A hard path the sages say, the sharp edge of a razor. He who knows the soundless, odorless, tasteless, intangible, formless, deathless, supernatural, undecaying, beginningless, endless, unchangeable Reality, springs out of the mouth of Death. . . .

"That which is here, is hereafter; hereafter is here. He who thinks otherwise wanders from death to death. . . . I will tell you the secret of undying Spirit and what happens after death. Some enter the womb, waiting for a moving body, some pass into unmoving things: according to deed and knowledge. . . . Through terror of God fire burns, sun shines, rain pours, wind blows, death speeds. Man, if he fail to find Him before the body falls, must take another body. . . . He who knows that the senses belong not to Spirit but to the elements, that they are born and die, grieves no more.

"Mind is above sense, intellect above mind, nature above intellect, the unmanifest above nature. Above the unmanifest is God, unconditioned, filling all things. He who finds Him enters immortal life, becomes free. No eye can see Him, nor has He a face that can be seen, yet through meditation and through discipline He can be found in the heart. He that finds Him enters immortal life. When mind and sense are at rest, when the discrimination of intellect is finished, man comes to his final condition. . . . When the desires of the heart are finished, man though still in the body is united to Spirit; mortal becomes immortal. When the knot of the heart is cut, mortal becomes immortal. This is the law.

"God, the inmost Self, no bigger than a thumb, lives in the heart. Man should strip him of the body, as the arrow-maker strips the reed, that he may know Him as perpetual and pure; what can He be but perpetual and pure?"

Then Nachiketas, having learnt from Death this knowledge, learnt the method of meditation, rose above desire and death, and found God.

# 3. THE ROMANCE OF DEATH

*"One would have to have a heart of stone," Oscar Wilde wickedly quipped, "not to read the death of Little Nell and laugh." Though they brought Victorian readers to tears, the portraits drawn by Charles Dickens (1812–70) of the deaths of children—especially Little Nell in* The Old Curiosity Shop *(1841) and Paul Dombey in* Dombey and Son *(1848)—did not age well for the Edwardian generation that followed. And yet, Dickens' portraits capture not only the particular Victorian sentimental fascination with both death and children, but also something people everywhere have observed: those who are dying, merely by the fact that they are dying, take on a moral significance and authority that only the most brutal can deny. In a debased form, it appears in the attempt of minor romantic fiction to make its characters interesting by giving them the pale faces of consumption. But in the hands of a master like Dickens, the romanticizing of death captures the awe that we feel when we face the dying.*

# Charles Dickens, *Dombey and Son*

Paul had never risen from his little bed. He lay there, listening to the noises in the street, quite tranquilly; not caring much how the time went, but watching it and watching everything about him with observing eyes.

When the sunbeams struck into his room through the rustling blinds, and quivered on the opposite wall like golden water, he knew that evening was coming on, and that the sky was red and beautiful. As the reflection died away, and a gloom went creeping up the wall, he watched it deepen, deepen, deepen into night. Then he thought how the long streets were dotted with lamps, and how the peaceful stars were shining overhead. His fancy had a strange tendency to wander to the river, which he knew was flowing through the great city; and now he thought how black it was, and how deep it would look, reflecting the hosts of stars—and more than all, how steadily it rolled away to meet the sea.

As it grew later in the night, and footsteps in the street became so rare that he could hear them coming, count them as they passed, and lose them in the hollow distance, he would lie and watch the many-colored ring about the candle, and wait patiently for day. His only trouble was, the swift and rapid river. He felt forced, sometimes, to try to stop it—to stem it with his childish hands—or choke its way with sand—and when he saw it coming on, resistless, he cried out! But a word from Florence, who was always at his side, restored him to himself, and leaning his poor head upon her breast, he told Floy of his dream, and smiled.

When day began to dawn again, he watched for the sun; and when its cheerful light began to sparkle in the room, he pictured to himself—pictured! he saw—the high church towers rising up into the morning sky, the town reviving, waking, starting into life once more, the river glistening as it rolled (but rolling fast as ever), and the country bright with dew. Familiar sounds and cries came by degrees into the street below; the servants in the house were roused and busy; faces looked in at the door, and voices asked his attendants softly how he was. Paul always answered for himself, "I am better. I am a great deal better, thank you! Tell Papa so!" By little and little, he got tired of the bustle of the day, the noise of carriages and carts, and people passing and repassing; and would fall asleep, or be troubled with a restless and uneasy sense again—the child could hardly tell whether this were in his sleeping or his waking moments—of that rushing river. "Why, will it never stop, Floy?" he would sometimes ask her. "It is bearing me away, I think!"

But Floy could always soothe and reassure him; and it was his daily delight to make her lay her head down on his pillow, and take some rest.

"You are always watching me, Floy. Let me watch *you,* now!" They would prop him up with cushions in a corner of his bed, and there he would recline the while she lay beside him: bending forward oftentimes to kiss her, and whispering to those who were near that she was tired, and how she had sat up so many nights beside him.

Thus, the flush of the day, in its heat and light, would gradually decline; and again the golden water would be dancing on the wall.

He was visited by as many as three grave doctors—they used to assemble downstairs, and come up together—and the room was so quiet, and Paul was so observant of them (though he never asked of anybody what they said), that he even knew the difference in the sound of their watches. But his interest centered in Sir Parker Peps, who always took his seat on the side of the bed. For Paul had heard them say long ago, that that gentleman had been with his mama when she clasped Florence in her arms, and died. And he could not forget it, now. He liked him for it. He was not afraid. . . .

How many times the golden water danced upon the wall; how many nights the dark, dark river rolled towards the sea in spite of him; Paul never counted, never sought to know. If their kindness, or his sense of it, could have increased, they were more kind, and he more grateful every day; but whether they were many days or few, appeared of little moment now, to the gentle boy.

One night he had been thinking of his mother, and her picture in the drawing-room down stairs, and thought she must have loved sweet Florence better than his father did, to have held her in her arms when she felt that she was dying—for even he, her brother, who had such dear love for her, could have no greater wish than that. The train of thought suggested to him to inquire if he had ever seen his mother; for he could not remember whether they had told him, yes or no, the river running very fast, and confusing his mind.

"Floy, did I ever see mama?"

"No, darling, why?"

"Did I ever see any kind face, like mama's, looking at me when I was a baby, Floy?"

He asked, incredulously, as if he had some vision of a face before him.

"Oh yes, dear!"

"Whose, Floy?"

"Your old nurse's. Often."

"And where is my old nurse?" said Paul. "Is she dead too? Floy, are we all dead, except you?"

There was a hurry in the room, for an instant—longer, perhaps; but it seemed no more—then all was still again; and Florence, with her face quite colorless, but smiling, held his head upon her arm. Her arm trembled very much.

"Show me that old nurse, Floy, if you please!"

"She is not here, darling. She shall come tomorrow."

"Thank you, Floy!"

Paul closed his eyes with those words, and fell asleep. When he awoke, the sun was high, and the broad day was clear and warm. He lay a little, looking at the windows, which were open, and the curtains rustling in the air, and waving to and ho: then he said, "Floy, is it tomorrow? Is she come?" . . .

Yes, yes. No other stranger would have shed those tears at sight of him, and called him her dear boy, her pretty boy, her own poor blighted child. No other woman would have stooped down by his bed, and taken up his wasted hand, and put it to her lips and breast, as one who had some right to fondle it. No other woman would have so forgotten everybody there but him and Floy, and been so full of tenderness and pity.

"Floy! this is a kind good face!" said Paul. "I am glad to see it again. Don't go away, old nurse! Stay here." . . .

Sister and brother wound their arms around each other, and the golden light came streaming in, and fell upon them, locked together.

"How fast the river runs, between its green banks and the rushes, Floy! But it's very near the sea. I hear the waves! They always said so!"

Presently he told her that the motion of the boat upon the stream was lulling him to rest. How green the banks were now, how bright the flowers growing on them, and how tall the rushes! Now the boat was out at sea, but gliding smoothly on. And now there was a shore before him. Who stood on the bank!—

He put his hands together, as he had been used to do at his prayers. He did not remove his arms to do it; but they saw him fold them so, behind her neck.

"Mama is like you, Floy. I know her by the face! But tell them that the print upon the stairs at school is not divine enough. The light about the head is shining on me as I go!"

The golden fipple on the wall came back again, and nothing else stirred in the room. The old, old fashion! The fashion that came in with our first garments, and will last unchanged until our race has run its course, and the wide firmament is rolled up like a scroll. The old, old fashion—Death!

Oh thank God, all who see it, for that older fashion yet, of Immortality! And look upon us, angels of young children, with regards not quite estranged, when the swift river bears us to the ocean!

# 4. WHERE ARE THE SNOWS OF YESTERYEAR?

*"Mother of God, where are they now? But where are the snows of yesteryear?" asks the fifteenth-century French poet Villon in his "Ballad of the Dead Ladies"—perhaps the most famous poem in an enormous genre of poetry known as the* Ubi Est? *("Where Is?"). The act of remembering the dead can invert the world of experience, and the absence and sheer pastness of the dead can suddenly seem more real than the present: as though ghosts had flesh and blood and the living world was only a shadow. In "Profundamente"—Portuguese for "profoundly"—the twentieth-century Brazilian poet Manuel Bandeira recounts a childhood memory of falling asleep and missing the street festival on the national holiday of St. John's Eve. Awakening too late, he looked out on the deserted square, the revelers all gone home. And suddenly, in adulthood, those days seem more real—and the sad experience of waking too late as a child becomes the heart-wrenching experience of missing the dead as an adult.*

# Manuel Bandeira, "Profundamente"

When I fell asleep last night
on Saint John's Eve
there was festival and clamor,
the rumble of fireworks, the flare of sparklers,
voices, songs, and laughter,
around the dancing bonfires.

In the middle of the night when I awoke
I could hear no more voices or laughter—
only erratic balloons drifting silently by,
only the distant clang of a streetcar
cutting the night like a tunnel.
Where were those who were dancing,
singing and laughing
around the fires?

—They were all sleeping,
They were all lying down,
sleeping
profoundly.

When I was six years old
I could not stay awake to see the end
of Saint John's Eve.
Today I hear no more
the voices of that day.
My grandmother,
my grandfather,
Totonio Rodrigues,
Tomasia,
Rosa,
where are they now?

—They are all sleeping,
they are all lying down,
sleeping
profoundly.

# 5. IN THE MIDST OF LIFE WE ARE IN DEATH

*Many of the most famous descriptions of death come from the sermons and poems of John Donne (1572–1631), the dean of St. Paul's Cathedral in London and greatest of the metaphysical poets. Written as he lay ill, hearing the bells of the nearby church toll the funerals of his neighbors, these lines from his 16th and 17th* Devotions Upon Emergent Occasions *remind us that death is all around us—and that the death of others is the loss of real parts of ourselves. And yet, Donne argues, it is precisely from considering these present deaths that we are led first to contemplate our own future death, and then to understand the necessity for faith in God who will preserve us from the void we cannot even imagine.*

# John Donne, *Devotions Upon Emergent Occasions*

From the bells of the church adjoining, I am daily remembered of my burial in the funerals of others. . . . I have lain near a steeple, in which there are said to be more than thirty bells, and near another, where there is one so big, as that the clapper is said to weigh more than six hundred pound; yet never so affected as here. Here the bells can scarce solemnize the funeral of any person, but that I knew him, or knew that he was my neighbor: we dwelt in houses near to one another before, but now he is gone into that house, into which I must follow him. . . .

We scarce hear of any man preferred, but we think of ourselves, that we might very well have been that man; why might not I have been that man, that is carried to his grave now? Could I fit myself to stand or sit in any man's place, and not to lie in any man's grave? I may lack much of the good parts of the meanest, but I lack nothing of the mortality of the weakest; they may have acquired better abilities than I, but I was borne to as many infirmities as they. To be an incumbent by lying down in a grave, to be a doctor by teaching mortification by example, by dying, though I may have seniors, others may be elder than I, yet I have proceeded apace in a good university, and gone a great way in a little time, by the furtherance of a vehement fever. . . .

Perchance he for whom this bell tolls, may be so ill, as that he knows not it tolls for him; and perchance I may think myself so much better than I am, as that they who are about me, and see my state, may have caused it to toll for me, and I know not that. The church is catholic, universal, so are all her actions; all that she does, belongs to all. When she baptizes a child, that action concerns me; for that child is thereby connected to that head which is my head too, and engrafted into that body, whereof I am a member. And when she buries a man, that action concerns me; all mankind is of one author, and is one volume; when one man dies, one chapter is not torn out of the book, but translated into a better language; and every chapter must be so translated; God employs several translators; some pieces are translated by age, some by sickness, some by war, some by justice; but God's hand is in every translation; and his hand shall bind up all our scattered leaves again, for that library where every book shall he open to one another: as therefore the bell that rings to a sermon, calls not upon the preacher only, but upon the congregation to come; so this bell calls us all: but how much more me, who am brought so near the door by this sickness. . . .

No man is an island, entire of itself, every man is a piece of the continent, a part of the main; if a clod be washed away by the sea, Europe is the less, as well as if a promontory were, as well as if a manor of thy friends, or of thine own were; any man's death diminishes me, because I am involved in mankind; and therefore never send to know for whom the bell tolls; it tolls for thee. Neither can we call this a begging of misery or a borrowing of misery, as though we were not miserable enough of our selves, but must fetch in more from the next house, in taking upon us the misery of our neighbors. Truly it were an excusable covetousness if we did (for affliction is a treasure and scarce any man hath enough of it). No man hath affliction enough, that is not matured, and ripened by it, and made fit for God by that affliction. . . . Tribulation is treasure in the nature of it, but it is not current money in the use of it, except we get nearer and nearer our home, heaven, by it. Another man may be sick too, and sick to death, and this affliction may lie in his bowels, as gold in a mine, and be of no use to him; but this bell that tells me of his affliction, digs out, and applies that gold to me: if by this consideration of another's danger, I take mine own into contemplation, and so secure myself, by making my recourse to my God, who is our only security.

# 6. THE MORALITY OF DEATH

*With her portrayals of Southern life as a grotesque blend of comedy and tragedy, Flannery O'Connor (1925–64) has become one of twentieth-century America's most widely admired authors. In her 1955 short story, "A Good Man Is Hard to Find," she succeeds at the nearly impossible task of conveying in fiction an illustration of the truth that death alone keeps us moral. Far from meaning that we may do as we like, the fact that we will die means that our choices have consequence—and that all we do is under judgment. The story opens with a Southern family on a car trip overtaken by an escaped criminal known only as The Misfit, and ends with the brutal declaration: " 'She would of been a good woman,' The Misfit said, 'if it had been somebody there to shoot her every minute of her life.' " Calling himself "The Misfit" because "I can't make what all I done wrong fit what all I gone through in punishment," he becomes in the story both the instrument of punishment for the grandmother and—like Jesus with the woman taken in adultery, drawing on the ground while he speaks with her—the instrument of her salvation.*

# Flannery O'Connor, "A Good Man Is Hard to Find"

"We've had an ACCIDENT!" the children screamed.

The grandmother had the peculiar feeling that the bespectacled man was someone she knew. His face was as familiar to her as if she had known him all her life but she could not recall who he was. He moved away from the car and began to come down the embankment, placing his feet carefully so that he wouldn't slip. He had on tan and white shoes and no socks, and his ankles were red and thin. "Good afternoon," he said. "I see you all had you a little spill."

"We turned over twice!" said the grandmother.

"Once," he corrected. "We seen it happen. Try their car and see will it run, Hiram," he said quietly to the boy with the gray hat.

"What you got that gun for?" John Wesley asked. "Whatcha gonna do with that gun?"

"Lady," the man said to the children's mother, "would you mind calling them children to sit down by you? Children make me nervous. I want all you all to sit down right together there where you're at."

"What are you telling US what to do for?" June Star asked. Behind them the line of woods gaped like a dark open mouth. "Come here," said their mother.

"Look here now," Bailey began suddenly, "we're in a predicament! We're in . . . "

The grandmother shrieked. She scrambled to her feet and stood staring. "You're The Misfit!" she said. "I recognized you at once!"

"Yes'm" the man said, smiling slightly as if he were pleased in spite of himself to be known, "but it would have been better for all of you, lady, if you hadn't of reckernized me."

Bailey turned his head sharply and said something to his mother that shocked even the children. The old lady began to cry and The Misfit reddened.

"Lady," he said, "don't you get upset. Sometimes a man says things he don't mean. I don't reckon he meant to talk to you thataway."

"You wouldn't shoot a lady, would you?" the grandmother said and removed a clean handkerchief from her cuff and began to slap at her eyes with it.

The Misfit pointed the toe of his shoe into the ground and made a little hole and then covered it up again. "I would hate to have to," he said.

"Listen," the grandmother almost screamed, "I know you're a good man. You don't look a bit like you have common blood. I know you must come from nice people!"

"Yes mam," he said, "finest people in the world." When he smiled he showed a row of strong white teeth. "God never made a finer woman than my mother and my daddy's heart was pure gold," he said. The boy with the red sweat shirt had come around behind them and was standing with his gun at his hip. The Misfit squatted down on the ground. "Watch them children, Bobby Lee," he said. "You know they make me nervous." He looked at the six of them huddled together in front of him and he seemed to be embarrassed as if he couldn't think of anything to say. "Ain't a cloud in the sky," he remarked, looking up at it. "Don't see no sun but don't see no cloud neither."

"Yes, it's a beautiful day," said the grandmother. "Listen," she said, "you shouldn't call yourself The Misfit because I know you're a good man at heart. I can just look at you and tell."

"Hush!" Bailey yelled. "Hush! Everybody shut up and let me handle this!" He was squatting in the position of a runner about to sprint forward but he didn't move.

"I pre-chate that, lady," The Misfit said and drew a little circle in the ground with the butt of his gun.

"It'll take a half a hour to fix this here car," Hiram called, looking over the raised hood of it.

"Well, first you and Bobby Lee get him and that little boy to step over yonder with you," The Misfit said, pointing to Bailey and John Wesley. "The boys want to ast you something," he said to Bailey. "Would you mind stepping back in them woods there with them?"

"Listen," Bailey began, "we're in a terrible predicament! Nobody realizes what this is," and his voice cracked. His eyes were as blue and intense as the parrots in his shirt and he remained perfectly still.

The grandmother reached up to adjust her hat brim as if she were going to the woods with him but it came off in her hand. She stood staring at it and after a second she let it fall on the ground. Hiram pulled Bailey up by the arm as if he were assisting an old man. John Wesley caught hold of his father's hand and Bobby Lee followed. They went off toward the woods and just as they reached the dark edge, Bailey turned and supporting himself against a gray naked pine trunk, he shouted, "I'll be back in a minute, Mamma, wait on me!"

"Come back this instant!" his mother shrilled but they all disappeared into the woods.

"Bailey Boy!" the grandmother called in a tragic voice but she found she was looking at The Misfit squatting on the ground in front of her. "I just know you're a good man," she said desperately. "You're not a bit common!"

"Nome, I ain't a good man," The Misfit said after a second as if he had considered her statement carefully, "but I ain't the worst in the world neither. My daddy said I was a different breed of dog from my brothers and sisters. 'You know,' Daddy said, 'it's some that can live their whole life out without asking about it and it's others has to know why it is, and this boy is one of the latters.

He's going to be into everything!'" He put on his black hat and looked up suddenly and then away deep into the woods as if he were embarrassed again. "I'm sorry I don't have on a shirt before you ladies," he said, hunching his shoulders slightly. "We buried our clothes that we had on when we escaped and we're just making do until we can get better. We borrowed these from some folks we met," he explained.

"That's perfectly all right," the grandmother said. "Maybe Bailey has an extra shirt in his suitcase."

"I'll look and see terrectly," The Misfit said.

"Where are they taking him?" the children's mother screamed.

"Daddy was a card himself," The Misfit said. "You couldn't put anything over on him. He never got in trouble with the Authorities though. Just had the knack of handling them."

"You could be honest too if you'd only try," said the grandmother. "Think how wonderful it would be to settle down and live a comfortable life and not have to think about somebody chasing you all the time."

The Misfit kept scratching in the ground with the butt of his gun as if he were thinking about it. "Yes'm, somebody is always after you," he murmured.

The grandmother noticed how thin his shoulder blades were just behind his hat because she was standing up looking down on him. "Do you ever pray?" she asked.

He shook his head. All she saw was the black hat wiggle between his shoulder blades. "Nome," he said.

There was a pistol shot from the woods, followed closely by another. Then silence. The old lady's head jerked around. She could hear the wind move through the tree tops like a long satisfied insuck of breath. "Bailey Boy!" she called.

"I was a gospel singer for a while," The Misfit said. "I been most everything. Been in the arm service, both land and sea, at home and abroad, been twict married, been an undertaker, been with the railroads, plowed Mother Earth, been in a tornado, seen a man burnt alive oncet," and he looked up at the children's mother and the little girl who were sitting close together, their faces white and their eyes glassy; "I even seen a woman flogged," he said.

"Pray, pray," the grandmother began, "pray, pray . . . "

"I never was a bad boy that I remember of," The Misfit said in an almost dreamy voice, "but somewheres along the line I done something wrong and got sent to the penitentiary. I was buried alive," and he looked up and held her attention to him by a steady stare.

"That's when you should have started to pray," she said. "What did you do to get sent to the penitentiary that first time?"

"Turn to the right, it was a wall," The Misfit said, looking up again at the cloudless sky. "Turn to the left, it was a wall. Look up it was a ceiling, look down it was a floor. I forget what I done, lady. I set there and set there, trying to remember what it was I done and I ain't recalled it to this day. Oncet in a while, I would think it was comin to me, but it never come."

"Maybe they put you in by mistake," the old lady said vaguely.

"Nome," he said. "It wasn't no mistake. They had the papers on me."

"You must have stolen something," she said.

The Misfit sneered slightly. "Nobody had nothing I wanted," he said. "It was a head-doctor at the penitentiary said what I had done was kill my daddy but I known that for a lie. My daddy died in nineteen ought nineteen of the epidemic flu and I never had a thing to do with it. He was buried in the Mount Hopewell Baptist churchyard and you can go there and see for yourself."

"If you would pray," the old lady said, "Jesus would help you."

"That's right," The Misfit said.

"Well then, why don't you pray?" she asked, trembling with delight suddenly.

"I don't want no hep," he said. "I'm doing all right by myself."

Bobby Lee and Hiram came ambling back from the woods. Bobby Lee was dragging a yellow shirt with bright blue parrots in it.

"Thow me that shirt, Bobby Lee," The Misfit said. The shirt came flying at him and landed on his shoulder and he put it on. The grandmother couldn't name what the shirt reminded her of. "No, lady," The Misfit said while he was buttoning it up, "I found out the crime don't matter. You can do one thing or you can do another, kill a man or take a tire off his car, because sooner or later you're going to forget what it was you done and just be punished for it."

The children's mother had begun to make heaving noises as if she couldn't get her breath. "Lady," he asked, "would you and that little girl like to step off yonder with Bobby Lee and Hiram and join your husband?"

"Yes, thank you," the mother said faintly. Her left arm dangled helplessly and she was holding the baby, who had gone to sleep, in the other. "Hep that lady up, Hiram," The Misfit said as she struggled to climb out of the ditch, "and Bobby Lee, you hold onto that little girl's hand."

"I don't want to hold hands with him," June Star said. "He reminds me of a pig."

The fat boy blushed and laughed and caught her by the arm and pulled her off into the woods after Hiram and her mother.

Alone with The Misfit, the grandmother found that she had lost her voice. There was not a cloud in the sky nor any sun. There was nothing around her but woods. She wanted to tell him that he must pray. She opened and closed her mouth several times before anything came out. Finally she found herself saying, "Jesus. Jesus," meaning, Jesus will help you, but the way she was saying it, it sounded as if she might be cursing.

"Yes'm," The Misfit said as if he agreed. "Jesus thown everything off balance. It was the same case with Him as with me except He hadn't committed any crime and they could prove I had committed one because they had the papers on me. Of course," he said, "they never shown me my papers. That's why I sign myself now. I said long ago, you get you a signature and sign everything you do and keep a copy of it. Then you'll know what you done and you can hold up the crime to the punishment and see do they match and in the end you'll have something to prove you ain't been treated right. I call myself The Misfit," he said, "because I can't make what all I done wrong fit what all I gone through in punishment."

There was a piercing scream from the woods, followed closely by a pistol report. "Does it seem right to you, lady, that one is punished a heap and another ain't punished at all?"

"Jesus!" the old lady cried. "You've got good blood! I know you wouldn't shoot a lady! I know you come from nice people! Pray! Jesus, you ought not to shoot a lady. I'll give you all the money I've got!"

"Lady," The Misfit said, looking beyond her far into the woods, "there never was a body that give the undertaker a tip."

There were two more pistol reports and the grandmother raised her head like a parched old turkey hen crying for water and called, "Bailey Boy, Bailey Boy!" as if her heart would break.

"Jesus was the only One that ever raised the dead," The Misfit continued, "and He shouldn't have done it. He thown everything off balance. If He did what He said, then it's nothing for you to do but thow away everything and follow Him, and if He didn't, then it's nothing for you to do but enjoy the few minutes you got left the best way you can—by killing somebody or burning down his house or doing some other meanness to him. No pleasure but meanness," he said and his voice had become almost a snarl.

"Maybe He didn't raise the dead," the old lady mumbled, not knowing what she was saying and feeling so dizzy that she sank down in the ditch with her legs twisted under her.

"I wasn't there so I can't say He didn't," The Misfit said. "I wisht I had of been there," he said, hitting the ground with his fist. "It ain't right I wasn't there because if I had of been there I would of known. Listen, lady," he said in a high voice, "if I had of been there I would of known and I wouldn't be like I am now." His voice seemed about to crack and the grandmother's head cleared for an instant. She saw the man's face twisted close to her own as if he were going to cry and she murmured, "Why you're one of my babies. You're one of my own children!" She reached out and touched him on the shoulder. The Misfit sprang back as if a snake had bitten him and shot her three times through the chest. Then he put his gun down on the ground and took off his glasses and began to clean them.

Hiram and Bobby Lee returned from the woods and stood over the ditch, looking down at the grandmother who half sat and half lay in a puddle of blood with her legs crossed under her like a child's and her face smiling up at the cloudless sky.

Without his glasses, The Misfit's eyes were red-rimmed and pale and defenseless-looking. "Take her off and thow her where you thown the others," he said, picking up the cat that was rubbing itself against his leg.

"She was a talker, wasn't she?" Bobby Lee said, sliding down the ditch with a yodel.

"She would of been a good woman," The Misfit said, "if it had been somebody there to shoot her every minute of her life."

"Some fun!" Bobby Lee said.

"Shut up, Bobby Lee," The Misfit said. "It's no real pleasure in life."

# 7. DEATH IN WAR

*"We would not die in that man's company, that fears ... to die with us,"*
*Shakespeare has Henry V declare before the Battle of Agincourt (1415),*
*where against overwhelming odds the English met and defeated the French*
*army. "What passing-bells for these who die as cattle?" Wilfred Owen*
*(1893–1918) returns in a poem written shortly before his death, at age*
*twenty-five, in the trenches of World War I—where battle seemed only filthy*
*and pointless. There is no middle ground between these two: Death in war*
*has always seemed both the most meaningful and the most meaningless*
*death one could suffer, the opportunity to die defending others and to die*
*defending nothing. So many of the themes that contemplation about death*
*must confront are present in such clear and sudden ways in war—fear and*
*glory, pain and honor, brutality and heroism—that much of the greatest art*
*and writing about death has taken the battlefield for its setting.*

# William Shakespeare, *Henry V*

*Westmoreland:* O! that we now had here
But one ten thousand of those men in England
That do not work to-day.

*King Henry:* What's he that wishes so!
My cousin Westmoreland? No, my fair cousin:
If we are mark'd to die, we are enough
To do our country loss; and if to live,
The fewer men, the greater share of honor.
God's will! I pray thee, wish not one man more.
By Jove, I am not covetous for gold,
Nor care I who doth feed upon my coat;
It yearns me not if men my garments wear;
Such outward things dwell not in my desires:

But if it be a sin to covet honor,
I am the most offending soul alive. . . .
God's peace! I would not lose so great an honor
As one man more, methinks, would share from me,
For the best hope I have. O! do not wish one more:
Rather proclaim it, Westmoreland, through my host,
That he which hath no stomach to this fight,
Let him depart; his passport shall be made,
And crowns for convoy put into his purse:

We would not die in that man's company
That fears his fellowship to die with us.
This day is call'd the feast of Crispian:
He that outlives this day, and comes safe home,
Will stand a-tiptoe when this day is named,
And rouse him at the name of Crispian.
He that shall live this day, and see old age;
Will yearly on the vigil feast his neighbors,
And say, "To-morrow is Saint Crispian."

Then will he strip his sleeve and show his scars,
And say, "These wounds I had on Crispin's day."

Old men forget; yet all shall be forgot,
But he'll remember with advantages
What feats he did that day. Then shall our names,
Familiar in his mouth as household words,
Harry the king, Bedford and Exeter,
Warwick and Talbot, Salisbury and Gloucester,
Be in their flowing cups freshly remembered.
This story shall the good man teach his son;

And Crispin Crispian shall ne'er go by,
From this day to the ending of the world,
But we in it shall be remembered;
We few, we happy few, we band of brothers;
For he to-day that sheds his blood with me
Shall be my brother; be he ne'er so vile
This day shall gentle his condition:
And gentlemen in England now abed
Shall think themselves accursed they were not here,
And hold their manhoods cheap whiles any speaks
That fought with us upon Saint Crispin's day.

# Wilfred Owen, "Anthem for Doomed Youth"

What passing-bells for these who die as cattle?
    Only the monstrous anger of the guns.
    Only the stuttering rifles' rapid rattle
Can patter out their hasty orisons.
No mockeries now for them; no prayers nor bells,
    Nor any voice of mourning save the choirs,—
The shrill, demented choirs of wailing shells;
And bugles calling for them from sad shires.

What candles may be held to speed them all?
    Not in the hands of boys, but in their eyes
Shall shine the holy glimmers of goodbyes.
    The pallor of girls' brows shall be their pall;
Their flowers the tenderness of patient minds,
And each slow dusk a drawing-down of blinds.

# 8. ACCEPTANCE BEYOND FEAR

*In the strict sense of the word, Stoicism is an ancient philosophical school—led, in its Roman form, by such writers as Seneca, Epictetus, and Marcus Aurelius—that emphasized detachment from fear and longing, resignation to fate, and faithful performance of the duties given to one in the world. In another sense, however, Stoicism is a perpetual opportunity for thought, a way of thinking about human life and death that has appeared in many different times and places. In this Renaissance passage, Michel de Montaigne (1533–92)—the creator and greatest master of the essay as a modern literary form—both presents classical Roman views on dying and adapts them for his own time. Arguing that clear knowledge of our coming death offers us not fear but freedom from fear, he urges his readers to keep death always in mind.*

# Montaigne, "To Philosophize Is to Learn to Die"

Cicero says "that to study philosophy is nothing but to prepare one's self to die." The reason is that study and contemplation do in some sort withdraw our soul and employ it separately from the body, which is a kind of apprenticeship and a resemblance of death; or else, because all the wisdom and reasoning in the world do in the end conclude in this point, to teach us not to fear to die. . . .

Of all the benefits that virtue confers upon us, the contempt of death is one of the greatest, as the means that accommodates human life with a soft and easy tranquillity, and gives us a pure and pleasant taste of living, without which all other pleasure would be extinct. . . . Death is inevitable, . . . and, consequently, if it frightens us, it is a perpetual torment, for which there is no sort of consolation. . . . Our courts of justice often send back condemned criminals to be executed upon the place where the crime was committed. But, if they were carried to fine houses by the way, prepared with the best entertainment, do you think they can relish it? That the fatal end of their journey being continually before their eyes, would not alter and deprave their palate from tasting these pleasures? . . .

The end of our race is death; it is the necessary object of our aim, which, if it frighten us, how is it possible to advance a step? The remedy the vulgar use is not to think on it; but from what brutish stupidity can they derive so gross a blindness? . . . I was born between eleven and twelve o'clock in the forenoon the last day of February, 1533 . . . and it is now just fifteen days since I was complete thirty-nine years; I make account to live, at least, as many more. In the meantime, to trouble a man's self with the thought of a thing so far off, were folly. But what? Young and old die upon the same terms; no one departs out of life otherwise than if he had but just before entered into it; neither is any man so old and decrepit, who, having heard of Methuselah, does not think he has yet twenty years good to come. Fool that thou art, who has assured unto thee the term of life? Thou dependest upon physicians' tales: rather consult effects and experience. According to the common course of things, it is long since that thou hast lived by extraordinary favor: thou hast already outlived the ordinary term of life. Reckon up your acquaintance: How many more have died before they arrived at thy age than have attained unto it? And of those who have ennobled their lives by their renown, take but an account, and I dare lay a wager thou wilt find more who have died before than after thirty-five years of age. . . .

Where death waits for us is uncertain; let us look for him everywhere. The premeditation of death is the premeditation of liberty; he who has learned to die, has unlearned to serve. There is nothing of evil in life, for him who rightly comprehends that the privation of life is no evil: to know how to die, delivers us from all subjection and constraint. . . .

For anything I have to do before I die, the longest leisure would appear too short, were it but an hour's business I had to do. . . . We should always, as near as we can, be booted and spurred, and ready to go, and, above all things, take care, at that time, to have no business with any one but one's self. We shall there find work enough to do, without any need of addition. One man complains, more than of death, that he is thereby prevented of a glorious victory, another, that he must die before he has married his daughter, or educated his children; a third seems only troubled that he must lose the society of his wife; a fourth, the conversation of his son, as the principal comfort and concern of his being. For my part, I am, thanks be to God, at this instant in such a condition, that I am ready to dislodge, whenever it shall please Him, without regret for anything whatsoever. . . . The deadest deaths are the best. . . .

To this purpose it was that men first appointed the places of sepulture adjoining the churches, and in the most frequented places of the city, to accustom, says Lycurgus, the common people, women, and children, that they should not be startled at the sight of a corpse, and to the end, that the continual spectacle of bones, graves, and funeral obsequies should put us in mind of our frail condition. . . . And as the Egyptians after their feasts were wont to present the company with a great image of death, by one that cried out to them, "Drink and be merry, for such shalt thou be when thou art dead." . . .

Perhaps some one may object, that the pain and terror of dying so infinitely exceed all manner of imagination, that the best fencer will be quite out of his play when it comes to the push. Let them say what they will: to premeditate is doubtless a very great advantage; and besides, is it nothing to go so far, at least, without disturbance or alteration? Moreover, nature herself assists and encourages us: if the death be sudden and violent, we have not leisure to fear; if otherwise, I perceive that as I engage further in my disease, I naturally enter into a certain loathing and disdain of life. . . .

Let us but observe in the ordinary changes and declinations we daily suffer, how nature deprives us of the light and sense of our bodily decay. What remains to an old man of the vigor of his youth and better days? . . . Caesar, to an old weather-beaten soldier of his guards, who came to ask him leave that he might kill himself, taking notice of his withered body and decrepit motion, pleasantly answered, "You fancy, then, that you are still alive." Should a man fall into this condition on the sudden, I do not think humanity capable of enduring such a change: but nature, leading us by the hand, an easy and, as it were, an insensible pace step by step conducts us to that miserable state, and by that means makes it familiar to us, so that we are insensible of the stroke when our youth dies in us, though it be really a harder death than the final dissolution of a languishing body, than the death of old age. . . .

Seeing we are threatened by so many sorts of death, is it not infinitely worse eternally to fear them all, than once to undergo one of them? And what matters it, when it shall happen, since it is inevitable? To him that told Socrates, "The thirty tyrants have condemned thee to death," Socrates replied, "And nature has condemned them." What a ridiculous thing it is to trouble ourselves about taking the only step that is to deliver us from all trouble! As our birth brought us the birth of all things, so in our death is the death of all things included. . . . Long life, and short, are by death made all one; for there is no long, nor short, to things that are no more. . . .

But nature compels us to it. "Go out of this world," says she, "as you entered into it; the same pass you made from death to life, without passion or fear, the same, after the same manner, repeat from life to death. Your death is a part of the order of the universe, it is a part of the life of the world. . . . Shall I exchange for you this beautiful contexture of things? It is the condition of your creation; death is a part of you, and while you endeavor to evade it, you evade yourselves. . . . All the whole time you live, you purloin from life, and live at the expense of life itself, . . . you are dead after life, but dying all the while you live; and death handles the dying much more rudely than the dead. . . . If you have lived a day, you have seen all: one day is equal and like to all other days. . . .

"Give place to others, as others have given place to you. Equality is the soul of equity. Who can complain of being comprehended in the same destiny, wherein all are involved? . . . Death is less to be feared than nothing, if there could be anything less than nothing. . . . Neither can it any way concern you, whether you are living or dead: living, by reason that you are still in being; dead because you are no more. Moreover, no one dies before his hour: the time you leave behind was no more yours than that was lapsed and gone before you came into the world. . . . Wherever your life ends, it is all there. The utility of living consists not in the length of days, but in the use of time; a man may have lived long, and yet lived but a little. Make use of time while it is present with you. It depends upon your will, and not upon the number of days, to have a sufficient length of life. . . . "

I have often considered with myself whence it should proceed, that in war the image of death, whether we look upon it in ourselves or in others, should, without comparison, appear less dreadful than at home in our own houses, and that . . . there should be much more assurance in peasants and the meaner sort of people, than in others of better quality. I believe, in truth, that it is those terrible ceremonies and preparations wherewith we set it out, that more terrify us than the thing itself; a new, quite contrary way of living; the cries of mothers, wives, and children; the visits of astounded and afflicted friends; the attendance of pale and blubbering servants; a dark room, set round with burning tapers; our beds environed with physicians and divines; in sum, nothing but ghastliness and horror round about us: we seem dead and buried already. Children are afraid even of those they are best acquainted with, when disguised in a visor, and so with us. The visor must be removed as well from things as from persons; that being taken away, we shall find nothing underneath but the very same death that a mean servant, or a poor chambermaid, died a day or two ago, without any manner of apprehension. Happy is the death that leaves us no leisure to prepare things for all this foolishness.

# 9. EAT, DRINK, AND BE MERRY

*Just as Stoicism is both a specific school of ancient philosophy and a way of thinking that has appeared in many different cultures, so forms of Epicureanism—technically, the school that follows the ancient Greek philosopher Epicurus—may be found again and again in history, a perpetual possibility for human thought about life and death. Omar Khayyám was an eleventh-century Persian poet and mathematician whose Rubáiyát puts in epigrammatical quatrains a view of life as containing nothing good but pleasure—and nothing so pleasurable as drunken conviviality. His work gave the Victorian poet Edward FitzGerald (1809–83) the opportunity to create this (not entirely faithful) paraphrase that found an enormous audience in Victorian England and America. Like Stoicism, Epicureanism urges us to keep death always in mind. Unlike Stoicism, however, it argues that the only reasonable response to death is the indulgence of whatever pleasures come our way.*

# Edward FitzGerald,
## *The Rubáiyát of Omar Khayyám*

They say the Lion and the Lizard keep
The Courts where Jamshyd gloried and drank deep;
    And Bahrám, that great Hunter—the Wild Ass
Stamps o'er his Head, but cannot break his Sleep.

I sometimes think that never blows so red
The Rose as where some buried Caesar bled;
    That every Hyacinth the Garden wears
Dropped in her Lap from some once lovely Head. . . .

And we, that now make merry in the Room
They left, and Summer dresses in new bloom,
    Ourselves must we beneath the Couch of Earth
Descend—ourselves to make a Couch—for whom? . . .

There was the Door to which I found no Key;
There was the Veil through which I might not see;
    Some little talk awhile of Me and Thee
There was—and then no more of Thee and Me. . . .

Then to the Lip of this poor earthen Urn
I leaned, the Secret of my Life to learn;
    And Lip to Lip it murmured—"While you live,
Drink!—for, once dead, you never shall return." . . .

You know, my Friends, with what a brave Carouse
I made a Second Marriage in my house,
    Divorced old barren Reason from my Bed,
And took the Daughter of the Vine to Spouse.

For "Is" and "Is-not" though with Rule and Line,
And "Up-and-down" by Logic, I define,
    Of all that one should care to fathom, I
Was never deep in anything but—Wine. . . .

I sent my Soul through the Invisible,
Some letter of that After-life to spell;
    And by and by my Soul returned to me,
And answered, "I Myself am Heav'n and Hell"—

Heaven but the Vision of fulfilled Desire,
And Hell the Shadow from a Soul on fire
    Cast on the Darkness into which Ourselves,
So late emerged from, shall so soon expire.

We are no other than a moving row
Of Magic Shadow-shapes that come and go
    Round with the Sun-illumined Lantern held
In Midnight by the Master of the Show;

But helpless Pieces of the Game He plays
Upon this Checkerboard of Nights and Days;
    Hither and thither moves, and checks, and slays,
And one by one back in the Closet lays. . . .

The Moving Finger writes, and, having writ,
Moves on; nor all your Piety nor Wit
    Shall lure it back to cancel half a Line,
Nor all your Tears wash out a Word of it. . . .

Ah, with the Grape my fading Life provide,
And wash the Body whence the Life has died,
    And lay me, shrouded in the living Leaf,
By some not unfrequented Garden-side. . . .

Ah, Love! could you and I with Him conspire
To grasp this sorry Scheme of Things entire,
    Would not we shatter it to bits—and then
Remold it nearer to the Heart's Desire! . . .

And when like her, O Sákí, you shall pass
Among the Guests Star-scattered on the Grass,
    And in your joyous errand reach the spot
Where I made One—turn down an empty Glass!

# 10. FATE AS THE WILL OF GOD (THE *QURAN*)

*Closely related to Stoicism and Epicureanism is Fatalism: the notion that everything that happens has been set to happen from the beginning of time, that humans only appear to have free will. In weak forms Fatalism appears in astrology and other attempts to discern the future through magical means. But in more sophisticated forms it appears both in certain schools of modern psychology (where any action we think we are free to undertake has actually been determined by our childhoods and environment), and in certain schools of theology (where expressing the power and foreknowledge of God becomes so important that the human will is at last denied). In the* Quran *(or Koran), the canonical book of Islam, Muhammad (570–632) shows how a general feeling of Fatalism may be transmuted into a theologically profound reverence for the Will of God—and death transmuted into the opportunity for participating in God's Judgment.*

*Islam offers a straightforward, some might say bleak, view of death and dying. Consider the following passage from* The Spectacle of Death *by Khawaja Muhammad Islam, under the title "This is the Reality of the World":*

May Almighty God be merciful to you! Be aware of your negligence and awaken yourselves from slumber before such time when a noise is heard that such a person has fallen ill; that his condition is precarious; that the physicians have been called in. The physicians and doctors will no doubt be called for you but no one will give you the guarantee of life. Then there will be a cry that he is making will. Look! His voice becomes inaudible. Now he is not recognizing anyone. He has started panting for breath. His groaning has increased. The eyelashes are drooping. This will be the moment when you will become well aware of the Hereafter, but your tongue would falter and you would not be able to say anything. The friends and relatives, standing there, will be weeping. Now, there appears before you your son, then comes your brother and lastly your wife. But the tongue has become speechless. In the meanwhile, every part of your body will start becoming lifeless and, at last, you will breathe your last and your soul will reach the heaven. Your kith and kin will make arrangments for your immediate burial. The visitors would observe silence after lamentation. Your enemies would rejoice. Your relatives would be absorbed in dividing the goods left behind by you while you are held accountable for your deeds.

This is the reality of mortal life.

*According to the* Quran, *which is understood to be the infallible revelation given Muhammad and correcting the partial revelations given earlier prophets such as Moses and Jesus, death is ordained by God but was from the beginning joined to the promise of bodily resurrection for those who are faithful to their islam, which means obedience to God. The purpose of death is to set a boundary on life's period of testing in which people are free (within the limits of God's will) to live according to the* sirat ulMustaqim, *which is the path that returns them to God, or to join the* kafirun, *the kafirs who reject God. Thus death is not a punishment but simply marks one stage along the way to resurrection and judgment. Islam teaches that those who die are visited by two angels, Munkar and Nakir, who ask them, "Whom have you worshipped and who is your prophet?" If they answer Allah and Muhammad, they rest until the Day of Judgment. Those who rejected Allah and Muhammad are immediately punished by the angels, either physically or by being shown the torments that await them after the judgment. This understanding is given forceful contemporary expression in the following passage from a contemporary description:*

Islam says, and the prophet of Islam has said, and the *Quran* has said, once a person dies and reaches into the grave, all of a sudden two angels appear and wake him up. His soul returns to the body. The very first question which is asked of the person, whether it's a man, woman or child, big or small, is: who is your God, what is your religion, who is your prophet? If the person has been good . . . what I have been told is this (because nobody has been into the grave; but we believe that what the prophet said is true—every single word is true; and what the Quran has said is that, because it is the Word of God, it's true): if the person has been good and has done the five prayers a day, once he opens his eyes in the grave, he would be looking at the sun as it is setting (because that's the time the two angels come), and he would think that he is dead and he is in the grave. He'd say, "Leave me alone." You see, the time of the third prayer comes exactly when the sun is setting. So he would say, "My prayer time is gone and I have overslept, so please let me pray." And if he has said that by the help of God, I don't think that the angels would bother him anymore—because he has answered every question. And if he hasn't done this, if he has been into the pubs and clubs and doing all the worldly things, and trying to snatch the things off anybody else, then the punishment would start from that very moment.

*Death is final and there is no second chance, although the unbelievers (kafirs) will plead to go back to life and try again. The days of resurrection and judgment are vividly described in the* Quran *in terms that are meant to be starkly literal and in no way figurative or allegorical. Bodies swarm out of the graves like locusts, a trumpet sounds, the heavens will be split open and the mountains levelled.*

So, when one blast is sounded on the trumpet, and the earth and the mountains are moved and are crushed to dust all in one blow, then on that day the happening will happen, and the sky will be rent asunder, for on that day it will be without strength; and the angels will be at its sides, and eight will bear the throne of your Lord above them on that day. That day you will be brought to judgment: none of your deeds that you hide will be hidden.

*Everything is written down most exactly in a book and every person will be held accountable for what he did or did not do in life. Unlike Christianity, Islam does not allow for any kind of redemption by which one person suffers on behalf of another. In fact, according to the* Quran, *Jesus did not die at all. God created a likeness of Jesus whom the Jews crucified. The* Quran *also warns against relying on the intercession of anyone else at the day of judgment. Every soul or life (nafs) must answer for itself.*

Ha! you are the ones who contend on their behalf in the present world. But who will contend with God on their behalf on the day of Resurrection, or who will be a guardian on their behalf? Whoever does evil or wrongs his own *nafs,* then seeks God's forgiveness, he will find God forgiving, merciful. And whoever earns a sin, earns it against his own *nafs;* and God is knowing, wise. And whoever earns a fault or a sin, then throws it on to one who is innocent, he has burdened himself with a falsehood and an open sin.

*The person's destination is either Heaven or Hell—or, as the* Quran *puts it, the Garden or the Fire. The Garden is depicted in graphic terms of endless delight:*

Surely, the righteous will be in a secure place, among gardens and springs. Dressed in silks and embroidered garments, they will enjoy each other's company—like that. And we will unite them with companions of wide eyes [*huri*]. They will ask there for every fruit, confidently. They will not taste death there, except the first death, and he will preserve them from the penalty of the blaze.

*The contrast with the Fire is equally graphic:*

Surely, those who reject our signs we will soon roast at the fire. As often as their skins are burnt through, we change them for other skins, that they may taste the penalty. Surely, God is powerful, wise. And those who believe and do deeds of righteousness we will cause to enter gardens with rivers flowing beneath, dwellers there for ever. There they will have companions unsullied, and we will bring them into the shade of shades.

*The entire process of death and judgment is foreshortened for the* shahid *(the witness) who is killed in the service of God. Longing for the status of witness (*talab ashShahada*) is therefore intense, and it can be attained either by violent death on behalf of Islam or by various forms of self-surrendering devotion. The entire teaching aims at inducing the utmost sobriety about the urgency of what is done in this life, as is evident in the following passage from* The Spectacle of Death:

In the Name of God, the Most Beneficent and Merciful
BEWARE

God alone is worthy of all praise, Who sent down death upon the greatest oppressors and the mightiest of men and wrigged their necks; and broke the backs of the greatest kings; and extinguished the hopes, the aspirations of the possessors of enormous hordes and treasures by putting an end to their lives, but when the promise of the Almighty (the time of death) came to pass, they were thrown into a pit and tumbled from their high palaces to the depths of the earth, they were lifted from their soft beds under the sparkle and glare of electric lights and were hurled into the darkness of the grave. They were engaged in dalliance with their slaves and handmaids when they were given over to the worms and insects, and instead of enjoying the delights of eating and drinking they were rolling in the dust; and they became lonely prisoners in the wilderness instead of enjoying the convivial society of friends.

*The drama of life, death, judgment, and reward is reflected in this short story from* The Spectacle of Death:

Musa b. Sima'k (mercy be upon him) says that Musa b. Mohammad b. Sulaiman Al-Hashmi was born with a silver spoon in his mouth. He was taken to the sensuous pleasures of life. The handsome boys and girls always absorbed his attention. He had neither any grief nor any anxiety to disturb him. He himself was the most beautiful man, handsome like a moon. He had all the amenities of life for him. His annual income was three lakhs and three thousand dinars annually which was entirely spent on swank living. He had a high balcony, with many windows opening towards the thorough-fare, through which he could see the people moving to and fro. And on the other side of his castle there were also many windows opening towards a garden through which he could enjoy the fragrance of the flowers. There was built a vault made of elephant's tusks fixed with silver nails and studded with a sheet of jewels. And that Hashmi had put on a turban on his head embellished with jewels. His friends and relatives were always seen gathered in that vault. The servants kept themselves standing behind them respectfully. In the front, there was always a troupe of female dancers and singers. Whenever he had a desire to listen to the songs, he used to cast a look at the guitar and all presented themselves before him, and when he desired to stop it, he did that by the gesture of his hand and the festivity came to an end. This state of affairs continued late at night till he was overwhelmed by sleep. When he, under the effect of intoxication, became senseless and his companions also went away, he caught any of the girls whom he liked and committed fornication with her the whole night. At dawn, he became busy in playing chess and chausar. Sorrow and anxiety, and death and sickness of any human being had no effect on him. He only knew merriment and laughter. Each day the new scents which were available at any place in that age were brought to him. Excellent bouquets of sweet-fragrant flowers were presented to him. In this state, he spent his twenty-seven years. At one night, he was in his apartment busy in enjoyments that he suddenly heard a very sweet voice which was quite different from that of his singers, but it was very fascinating. No sooner did he hear that voice than he began to feel uneasy. He ordered his singing girls to stop singing, and began to hear that voice by stretching out his head outside the window of his room. For some moments that voice remained audible and then stopped. He ordered his servants to bring the man before him whose voice he had been hearing. The cups of wine were rotating in the company. The servants ran out hurriedly in the direction whence the voice was coming and entered into a mosque, where they found a young man standing in a corner of the mosque and talking to his Lord. He was pale and weak. His neck was slender; his lips dry. His hair was dirty and his belly pressed in. He had put on two sheets of a cloth, which hardly covered his body. These people caught hold of him and nothing was said or told to him. Within no time, they removed him from the mosque and produced him before that Hashmi who was sitting in that balcony and they said: "Here he is, Sir." He, being under the influence of wine, said: "Who is he?" They begged and told him: "He is that man the voice of whom you had heard." He asked them: "From which place have you brought him here?" They told him that he was in a mosque. He was standing and reciting the Holy *Quran*. That rich man asked the young saint: "What were you reciting?" He said: "A'auzobillah" and then recited some verses of the Holy *Quran* from Surah at-Tatfif (Defrauding), the translation of which is given below: —

"Lo! the righteous verily are in delight, on couches, gazing. Thou wilt know in their face the radiance of delight. They are given to drinking of pure wine which is sealed. Whose seal is musk—For this let (all) those strive for bliss—And mixed with water of Tasnim, a spring whence those brought near to Allah drink."

Thus, those who are jealous of others' fortune, should be greedy for such things (and be anxious to get more blessings by good deeds and, as such, we should vie with each other in those deeds by which we can be favoured with these blessings). And that wine will be mixed with the water of Tasnim (if something is mixed with wine, its potency is increased) and that Tasnim is a spring in the Heaven whence those brought near to Allah drink. Those who are near to Allah will get pure water from this spring and some water will be mixed from this spring with the wine to be given to pious men.

After this, the poor young man said: "O you who are deceived: Your palace, this high balcony and carpets! these have no comparison with them whatsoever."

Those are raised couches upon which carpets are spread. Those are very high couches. Their couches are lined with silk brocade. Those people are reclining on green cushions and fair carpets. The friend of Allah, sitting on these couches will see two such ever bubbling springs which will be playing between two gardens. In these two gardens, there is every kind of fruit in pairs. Every kind of fruit will have two different tastes. Those fruits will neither be perishing nor will there be any restriction for plucking them (as we are prohibited to pluck them in the world by the gardener). These people will be in a blissful state in a high garden. They will be in such a high garden where they hear no idle speech; wherein is a gushing spring; wherein couches are raised; and goblets set at hand; and cushions ranged; and silken carpets spread. Those people are amid shade and fountains. The fruits of its Garden are everlasting, and its shade also; this is the reward of those who keep their duty, while the reward of disbelievers is the Fire. How much painful that fire will be. (May God protect us from that.) Lo! the guilty are immortal in hell's torment. It is not relaxed for them, and they despair therein. Lo! the guilty are in error and madness. On the day when they are dragged into the Fire upon their faces (it is said unto them) feel the touch of hell. Those people will be in fire, in boiling water and shadow of black smoke. The guilty man will long to rescue himself from the punishment of that day at the even price of his children, and his spouse and his brother, and his kin that harboured him, and all that are in the earth, if then it might deliver him. But nay for lo! it is the fire of hell, eager to roast! it calleth him who turned and fled (from truth); and hoarded (wealth) and withheld it.

Such a man will be in a great torture and in a painful doom; he will be a victim of Almighty God's anger; he will be in everlasting doom.

In this discourse, the young pious man has alluded to numerous verses of the Holy *Quran,* relating to Heaven and Hell, and has also made references to Surahs of the Holy *Quran* from where these have been quoted.

On listening to the discourse of the young pious man, the rich Hashmi stood up from his seat and embraced him and began to weep loudly. He said to all his companions to go away and then took the young saint with him in the courtyard and sat on a rough mat; there he lamented over his youth and kept on weeping for his past state of affairs and the young saint was busy in imparting lessons to him till it was dawn. In the first instance, he repented for his sins in the presence of the young saint and made a solemn pledge before Almighty God in a corner of the mosque. He sold all his belongings and all his goods and spent their proceeds on the welfare of the public. He dismissed all his servants. He returned all those things which he had appropriated unjustly to the real owners of them. He freed most of his servants and handmaids, and most of them were sold by him and their price spent in the welfare of the public. He put on rough clothes. He began to eat barley bread. The whole night he worshipped God and during the day kept fast. At last, the saint and pious people began to visit him. He showed such keenness in the worship of God that people begged him to take pity on himself and not to burden his being with an unbearable burden. He instructed him that Almighty God is the most Beneficent and giveth a great reward for a little effort. But he used to say: "O friends! Only I know in what position I am. I disobeyed my God day and night. I committed many a major and minor sins." After saying this, he kept on weeping and wept bitterly. In this condition, he walked towards Mecca barefooted for the performance of Pilgrimage (Hajj). He had put on a thick cloth on his body. He had with him one bowl and a bag only. In this condition, he reached Mecca and after the performance of Hajj, he stayed there till the end of his life (may mercy be upon him). During his stay at Mecca, he went in "Hatim" and wept vehemently, implored humbly and earnestly and used to say: "O my Lord! I have passed many of my solitudes but never cared about Thee. I annoyed Thee with horrible sins. My Lord! I have lost all my goods. (I have gained nothing.) There is a burden of sins upon me now. There will be destruction for me on the day (The Day of Judgment) when I will be meeting with Thee. In other words, there is ruin upon ruin for me, that is, a great destruction on the day when my scroll will be opened before me. Ah! That will be filled with wicked deeds and sins committed by me, but ruin has befallen me because of Thine anger and Thine anger is a destruction for me which is due to my defiant attitude towards Thee and for misusing the favours and blessings Thou showered upon me. And Thou were seeing all this disobedience of mine. O my Lord! There is no place for shelter for me, except Thee, where I may find escape. There is none save Thee to beseech. There is none save Thee to trust in. My Lord! I am not in a position to pray Thee for heaven but I pray Thee in the name of Thy Kindness, Forgiveness and Thy Grace to take pity on me and forgive me my sins."

"These are the people who are near to Allah and who are forgiven."

Hadrat Malik b. Dinar (mercy be upon him) says: "I was on my way to Mecca for the performance of Hajj when I saw a young boy walking on foot. He had neither any conveyance, nor provision for the journey, nor water. I paid him salutations which he readily responded." I said: "O young boy whence are you coming?" He told me: "From Him (God)." I again asked him about his destination, to which he replied that he was returning to God. I asked him: "Where is your provision for the journey?" He told: "This is up to Him (God) to provide me that." I told him: "It is impossible to cover this journey without provision of meal and water. Don't you have something with you?" The young boy replied: "I had, at the outset of my journey, some words as the provision for journey." I asked him: "Which are those five words?" He told me: "These are: Ka'f-ha'-ya'-ain-s—the holy commandments of Almighty God." He further explained the meanings of these five words as under:—

(1) Ka'f—The Sufficient;
(2) Ha'—The Guide;
(3) Ya'—The Protector;
(4) 'Ain—Knower of all things; and
(5) S—The True—True to his promise.

Thus a man, the companion of whom is One Who is Sufficient, the unerring Guide, the Protector, the Knower of all things and the True (True to His words), can ever be ruined or entertained any fear? Can such a person bother for the carriage of provision and water during the course of his journey? Hadrat Malik (mercy be upon him) says: "I wanted to give the young boy my shirt but he refused to take it and said: 'O aged man! Is it not better to be bare than to get a shirt?' He further said: 'In the Hereafter, we will be answerable for the permissible things of the world and will have to suffer punishment for the forbidden things of the world.'" When the darkness of night spread over, the young boy turned his face towards the sky and prayed to Allah Who is pleased when His bondsmen obey Him, and suffers no loss if His bondsmen disobey Him, by uttering these words: "O God! Favour me with that thing by which Thou art pleased, that is, Obedience, and forgive me that thing which causeth Thou no loss, that is Sin." After this, the people put on their 'Ihram' (pilgrims' dress) and began to recite the words: "Here I am to do Thy bidding my Lord!" But the young boy was silent. I asked him: "Why don't you declare, 'Here I am to do Thy bidding my Lord!'?" He told: "I fear if I say: 'Here I am to do Thy bidding my Lord'; the reply may be: 'I neither hear your talk nor pay any attention towards you.'" Then he went away. After this, he was not seen during the journey. At last, he was seen in *Mina* where he recited some poetic verses, the translation of which is given as under:—

"The Beloved, Who is keen to shed my blood, has every right to shed my blood in haram or outside haram. By God! If my soul comes to know with Whom it is related, it may stand headlong instead on foot. O censurer! Do not censure me for being entangled in His love. If you happen to see what I am seeing, you never dare to talk like this. The people make a circuit of the holy Ka'ba bodily and, if they make a circuit of Exalted God, there will be no need for them of the 'Haram.' On the day of 'Id the people sacrificed sheep and goats in the way of Allah but the lover of Allah sacrificed his life in His way. The people have performed the Hajj but my Hajj is that I have been able to get tranquility. The people have sacrficed sheep and goats but I sacrifice my blood and soul. After this, he prayed: 'O God! The people have gained access to thee by sacrifices. I have nothing to sacrifice save my soul. I offer it to Thee for acceptance.'"

Thereupon he screamed and fell down as dead. After this incident, a hidden voice was heard: "He is the companion of Allah. He is a martyr in the cause of Allah."

Hadrat Malik (mercy be upon him) says: "I performed the burial of the young boy and remained anxious and thoughtful about him the whole night. In the meantime, I fell asleep and saw him in the dream." I asked him: "What happened to you?" He told: "As had happened with the martyrs."

# 11. THE PHENOMENON OF HOPE

*In contrast to John Donne's analysis of the death of others bringing us to knowledge of our own death, Dietrich von Hildebrand (1889–1977) argues that there is a fundamental difference between grief and the fear of death. A convert to Catholicism in his twenties, von Hildebrand was teaching philosophy in Munich when Hitler came to power. Refusing to live in a country "ruled by a criminal," he moved to Austria where he led the fight against Nazism. Pursued by German assassins, he fled to the United States, where he taught philosophy at Fordham University until his retirement. Written when the author was eighty-six years old and in declining health,* Jaws of Death, Gate of Heaven *uses the twentieth-century philosophical method of phenomenology to seek the grounds for belief in immortality: In the experience of genuine love for another human being, we find ourselves compelled to believe in the God who will preserve the one we love from nothingness and non-being.*

# Dietrich von Hildebrand,
## *Jaws of Death, Gate of Heaven*

My love can look beyond death and somehow know that my beloved cannot really die. . . . This points to everything that touches on the immortality of the soul, everything that asserts the impossibility of my loved one's merely fading away even though her body has ceased to live. Many things indeed point to immortality and, once the existence of God is admitted, even give proof of it. This indication is nowhere so pronounced—nowhere so strong and vibrant—as in the ultimate love I feel for my precious beloved. It is, in fact, my own strong love which cries out, "You shall not die!"

But even this awareness of immortality does not remove the dread of death, does not neutralize its sting. The frightfulness of separation remains; an empty loneliness gapes at me. . . . I know indeed that the physiological processes are essentially different from those of the soul. I even accept the many clear hints of immortality and thus am convinced of the continued existence of my beloved's soul. But I yet must stare at the brutal event of her body's dissolution; I am faced with the fundamental difference between her living body and her lifeless corpse.

Even if on the natural plane I am convinced that her soul has not ceased to exist, I nonetheless am constrained to ask, "Where is she?" She had in former times stood before me. I could see her dear face, her lovely form. I was able to speak to her and she was able to reply to my questions and to respond to the expression of my love. She could surprise me in her answers; her words could go far beyond anything I had expected in the way of love.

Now everything is quiet. I can no longer reach her. A frightful emptiness surrounds me. Everything I encounter impresses me with the contrast between visible, earthly reality and the puzzling absence of the one I love. I have lost the one human person loved by me without measure or comparison. I am caught up now in the tedium of life. I am filled with disgust and emptiness over the rhythm of everyday life that goes on relentlessly—as though nothing had changed, as though I had not lost my precious beloved!

Compared to the death of my beloved, what are all other evils and sufferings of life? This vale of tears certainly has for us a vast number and variety of sorrows—from loss of sight and the serious pains that rack our body to imprisonment in a concentration camp and the dreadful sufferings entailed by such a fate. But the loss of a beloved person follows a different course. It does not involve bodily sufferings, nor the loss of the obviously good things of life. No, the death of my beloved concerns an incredibly blissful, purely positive treasure. It marks the end of a natural spring of joy.

We touch here upon the sinister fate of all human beings: death, which hangs like the sword of Damocles over every human life. Each of us lives *in umbra mortis*, in the dread shadow of death. Compared to the death of someone I love, all other sufferings are merely incidental. Death threatens each of us essentially; no one is exempt. I am constantly aware that my beloved comes closer to death with each passing day. I know that death may snatch her away tomorrow.

Someone who has never known an ultimate love in this life, who has never given his heart to another human who has loved him in return, knows nothing of the fundamental horror with which the death of a beloved person surrounds us.

Now lifeless in shape is my loved one's body which had been always included in my love (even in that non-marital form of love in which the intention of union does not aim at corporal union). Her body which formerly was filled with the nobility of her precious personality is now subject to a dreadful kind of decay and decomposition. Her soul has vanished into an unattainable distance and is radically cut off from us. My incomprehensible, puzzling dread of death remains in its natural aspect despite my conviction that her soul continues to exist.

St. Augustine speaks in a unique way in his *Confessions* of the night of suffering into which he was plunged by the death of his friend: "At this grief, my heart was utterly darkened, and whatever I beheld was death. My native country was a torment to me, and my father's house a strange unhappiness; and whatever I had shared with him, wanting him, became a distracting torture. Mine eyes sought him everywhere, but he was not granted them; and I hated all places, for that they had not him; nor could they now tell me, 'he is coming,' as when he was alive and absent. I became a great riddle to myself, and I asked my soul why she was so sad and why she disquieted me sorely: but she knew not what to answer me."

Seeing death as a happy liberation from the prison of the body (an idea which Socrates defends) makes sense only for my own death, but never for the death of a dearly beloved person. When I mentally anticipate my own death *ante mortem*—before my death—I do not experience that bewildering loneliness, that heart-breaking contrast between the unimportant things that go on living and the bleak present, now that the light of my beloved has ceased to shine.

In the case of my own death, love retreats entirely into the background. But the death of my beloved overwhelms me *post mortem*—after her death. The joy I once knew in her living presence is replaced by the horror of separation, by the dread of death as the great enemy of love and human happiness. . . .

Quite different is the case where the longing for death is motivated by spiritual despair about the world or about life as a whole. Thus the young Jacques Maritain and his wife, Raissa, were in such despair over the philosophical teachings of the positivists at the Sorbonne concerning the relativity of all truth, that they decided to take their own lives. A life without the possibility of absolute truth seemed to them not worth living.

They had already agreed on the day and the hour of their mutual suicides when they met with the teaching and personality of the eminent philosopher, Henri Bergson. He convinced them that objective truth exists. He gave them hope of discovering it. For the Maritains before they met Bergson, therefore, as well as for all those who seek death for similar reasons, death means the cessation—not of intolerable sufferings in this life—but of life itself. . . .

The longing for death has still a different character when it is a response to the death of someone we love very deeply. Death itself takes on a different hue in each of its several aspects. In this instance, we may long for death because the worst and most frightful natural misfortune has befallen us. From the natural point of view, we are afflicted with the greatest and deepest loss possible to humans. This particular yearning for death has an especially noble character, born of love and of love's tears and grief. . . . Our beloved is dead. Our bereavement, from the natural point of view, does really call for an anguished yearning for radical relief when bereavement is the motive, our yearning for death is also implicitly bound up with our certainty about the continued existence of the soul in the life beyond. This yearning, in fact, presupposes the belief that there shall be a reunion with our beloved in eternity.

# 12. THE IRREPLACEABLE DEAD

*The Welsh poet Dylan Thomas (1914–53) wrote as many well-known lines about death as anyone in the twentieth century, including his famous villanelle for his dying father, "Do not go gentle into that good night." Sense in Thomas often seems subordinate to the melody of his words, and he has the reputation of being a difficult but almost mesmerizing poet. In "A Refusal to Mourn the Death, by Fire, of a Child in London," he extends through his strange, sound-driven images an argument that each dead person is so unique, so irreplaceable, and so lost to us that all we can do is record the sheer fact of it: "After the first death, there is no other."*

# Dylan Thomas, "A Refusal to Mourn the Death, by Fire, of a Child in London"

Never until the mankind making
Bird beast and flower
Fathering and all humbling darkness
Tells with silence the last light breaking
And the still hour
Is come of the sea tumbling in harness

And I must enter again the round
Zion of the water bead
And the synagogue of the ear of corn
Shall I let pray the shadow of a sound
Or sow my salt seed
In the least valley of sackcloth to mourn

The majesty and burning of the child's death.
I shall not murder
The mankind of her going with a grave truth
Nor blaspheme down the stations of the breath
With any further
Elegy of innocence and youth.

Deep with the first dead lies London's daughter,
Robed in the long friends,
The grains beyond age, the dark veins of her mother,
Secret by the unmourning water
Of the riding Thames.
After the first death, there is no other.

# Part II

# WHEN WE DIE

# 1. THE EXPERIENCE OF DEATH

*"My death," the twentieth-century philosopher Ludwig Wittgenstein once declared, "is not an event in my life"—for we can never "experience" being dead. Nonetheless, death touches us at two moments: when others die and while we are dying. Though we cannot experience being dead, we will experience the process of dying. Perhaps the most persuasive imaginative portrayal of this dying is the one given in* The Death of Ivan Ilych, *a story composed in 1886 by Count Leo Tolstoy (1828–1910). If we cannot know exactly what dying will be like until we ourselves go through it, we have certain intuitions about it from sickness, grief and religious prophecy, and Tolstoy's account of the dying Ilych gives convincing expression to those intuitions. The unearned care and undeserved indifference of the living, the pain and release from pain, the vital importance of the body and the soul's gradual detachment from it, all find their clear expression in the story, as Tolstoy builds—from our intuitions about dying—a case for the expectation of immortality.*

# Leo Tolstoy, *The Death of Ivan Ilych*

His wife returned late at night. She came in on tiptoe, but he heard her, opened his eyes, and made haste to close them again. She wished to send Gerasim away and to sit with him herself, but he opened his eyes and said: "No, go away."

"Are you in great pain?"

"Always the same."

"Take some opium."

He agreed and took some. She went away.

Till about three in the morning he was in a state of stupefied misery. It seemed to him that he and his pain were being thrust into a narrow, deep black sack, but though they were pushed further and further in they could not be pushed to the bottom. And this, terrible enough in itself, was accompanied by suffering. He was frightened yet wanted to fall through the sack, he struggled but yet co-operated. And suddenly he broke through, fell, and regained consciousness. Gerasim was sitting at the foot of the bed dozing quietly and patiently, while he himself lay with his emaciated stockinged legs resting on Gerasim's shoulders; the same shaded candle was there and the same unceasing pain.

"Go away, Gerasim," he whispered.

"It's all right, sir. I'll stay a while."

"No. Go away."

He removed his legs from Gerasim's shoulders, turned sideways onto his arm, and felt sorry for himself. He only waited till Gerasim had gone into the next room and then restrained himself no longer but wept like a child. He wept on account of his helplessness, his terrible loneliness, the cruelty of man, the cruelty of God, and the absence of God.

"Why hast Thou done all this? Why hast Thou brought me here? Why, why dost Thou torment me so terribly?"

He did not expect an answer and yet wept because there was no answer and could be none. The pain again grew more acute, but he did not stir and did not call. He said to himself: "Go on! Strike me! But what is it for? What have I done to Thee? What is it for?"

Then he grew quiet and not only ceased weeping but even held his breath and became all attention. It was as though he were listening not to an audible voice but to the voice of his soul, to the current of thoughts arising within him.

"What is it you want?" was the first clear conception capable of expression in words, that he heard.

"What do you want? What do you want?" he repeated to himself.

"What do I want? To live and not to suffer," he answered. And again he listened with such concentrated attention that even his pain did not distract him.

"To live? How?" asked his inner voice.

"Why, to live as I used to—well and pleasantly."

"As you lived before, well and pleasantly?" the voice repeated.

And in imagination he began to recall the best moments of his pleasant life. But strange to say none of those best moments of his pleasant life now seemed at all what they had then seemed—none of them except the first recollections of childhood. There, in childhood, there had been something really pleasant with which it would be possible to live if it could return. But the child who had experienced that happiness existed no longer, it was like a reminiscence of somebody else.

As soon as the period began which had produced the present Ivan Ilych, all that had then seemed joys now melted before his sight and turned into something trivial and often nasty.

And the further he departed from childhood and the nearer he came to the present the more worthless and doubtful were the joys. This began with the School of Law. A little that was really good was still found there—there was light-heartedness, friendship, and hope. But in the upper classes there had already been fewer of such good moments. Then during the first years of his official career, when he was in the service of the governor, some pleasant moments again occurred: they were the memories of love for a woman. Then all became confused and there was still less of what was good; later on again there was still less that was good, and the further he went the less there was. His marriage, a mere accident, then the disenchantment that followed it, his wife's bad breath and the sensuality and hypocrisy: then that deadly official life and those preoccupations about money, a year of it, and two, and ten, and twenty, and always the same thing. And the longer it lasted the more deadly it became. "It is as if I had been going downhill while I imagined I was going up. And that is really what it was. I was going up in public opinion, but to the same extent life was ebbing away from me. And now it is all done and there is only death.

"Then what does it mean? Why? It can't be that life is so senseless and horrible. But if it really has been so horrible and senseless, why must I die? And die in agony? There is something wrong!"

"Maybe I did not live as I ought to have done," it suddenly occurred to him. "But how could that be, when I did everything properly?" he replied, and immediately dismissed from his mind this, the sole solution of all the riddles of life and death, as something quite impossible.

"Then what do you want now? To live? Live how? Live as you lived in the law courts when the usher proclaimed 'The judge is coming!' The judge is coming, the judge!" he repeated to himself "Here he is, the judge. But I am not guilty!" he exclaimed angrily. "What is it for?" And he ceased crying, but turning his face to the wall continued to ponder on the same question: Why, and for what purpose, is there all this horror? But however much he pondered he found no answer. And whenever the thought occurred to him, as it often did, that it all resulted from his not having lived as he ought to have done, he at once recalled the correctness of his whole life and dismissed so strange an idea.

Another fortnight passed. Ivan Ilych now no longer left his sofa. He would not lie in bed but lay on the sofa, facing the wall nearly all the time. He suffered ever the same unceasing agonies and in his loneliness pondered always on the same insoluble question: "What is this? Can it be that it is Death?" And the inner voice answered: "Yes, it is Death."

"Why these sufferings?" And the voice answered, "For no reason—they just are so." Beyond and besides this there was nothing.

From the very beginning of his illness, ever since he had first been to see the doctor, Ivan Ilych's life had been divided between two contrary and alternating moods: now it was despair and the expectation of this uncomprehended and terrible death, and now hope and an intently interested observation of the functioning of his organs. Now before his eyes there was only a kidney or an intestine that temporarily evaded its duty, and now only that incomprehensible and dreadful death from which it was impossible to escape.

These two states of mind had alternated from the very beginning of his illness, but the further it progressed the more doubtful and fantastic became the conception of the kidney, and the more real the sense of impending death.

He had but to call to mind what he had been three months before and what he was now, to call to mind with what regularity he had been going downhill, for every possibility of hope to be shattered.

Latterly during the loneliness in which he found himself as he lay facing the back of the sofa, a loneliness in the midst of a populous town and surrounded by numerous acquaintances and relations but that yet could not have been more complete anywhere—either at the bottom of the sea or under the earth—during that terrible loneliness Ivan Ilych had lived only in memories of the past. Pictures of his past rose before him one after another. They always began with what was nearest in time and then went back to what was most remote—to his childhood—and rested there. If he thought of the stewed prunes that had been offered him that day, his mind went back to the raw shriveled French plums of his childhood, their peculiar flavor and the flow of saliva when he sucked their stones, and along with the memory of that taste came a whole series of memories of those days: his nurse, his brother, and their toys. "No, I mustn't think of that. . . . It is too painful," Ivan Ilych said to himself, and brought himself back to the present—to the button on the back of the sofa and the creases in its morocco. "Morocco is expensive, but it does not wear well: there had been a quarrel about it. It was a different kind of quarrel and a different kind of morocco that time when we tore father's portfolio and were punished, and mamma brought us some tarts. . . . " And again his thoughts dwelt on his childhood, and again it was painful and he tried to banish them and fix his mind on something else.

Then again together with that chain of memories another series passed through his mind—of how his illness had progressed and grown worse. There also the further back he looked the more life there had been. There had been more of what was good in life and more of life itself. The two merged together. "Just as the pain went on getting worse and worse, so my life grew worse and worse," he thought. "There is one bright spot there at the back, at the beginning of life, and afterwards all becomes blacker and blacker and proceeds more and more rapidly—in inverse ratio to the square of the distance from death," thought Ivan Ilych. And the example of a stone falling downwards with increasing velocity entered his mind. Life, a series of increasing sufferings, flies further and further towards its end—the most terrible suffering. "I am flying. . . . " He shuddered, shifted himself, and tried to resist, but was already aware that resistance was impossible, and again with eyes weary of gazing but unable to cease seeing what was before them, he stared at the back of the sofa and waited—awaiting that dreadful fall and shock and destruction.

"Resistance is impossible!" he said to himself. "If I could only understand what it is all for! But that too is impossible. An explanation would be possible if it could be said that I have not lived as I ought to. But it is impossible to say that," and he remembered all the legality, correctitude, and propriety of his life. "That at any rate can certainly not be admitted," he thought, and his lips smiled ironically as if someone could see that smile and be taken in by it. "There is no explanation! Agony, death. . . . What for?"

Another two weeks went by in this way and during that fortnight an event occurred that Ivan Ilych and his wife had desired. Petrishchev formally proposed. It happened in the evening. The next day Praskovya Fedorovna came into her husband's room considering how best to inform him of it, but that very night there had been a fresh change for the worse in his condition. She found him still lying on the sofa but in a different position. He lay on his back, groaning and staring fixedly straight in front of him.

She began to remind him of his medicines, but he turned his eyes towards her with such a look that she did not finish what she was saying; so great an animosity, to her in particular, did that look express.

"For Christ's sake let me die in peace!" he said.

She would have gone away, but just then their daughter came in and went up to say good morning. He looked at her as he had done at his wife, and in reply to her inquiry about his health said dryly that he would soon free them all of himself. They were both silent and after sitting with him for a while went away.

"Is it our fault?" Lisa said to her mother. "It's as if we were to blame! I am sorry for papa, but why should we be tortured?"

The doctor came at his usual time. Ivan Ilych answered "Yes" and "No," never taking his angry eyes from him, and at last said: "You know you can do nothing for me, so leave me alone."

"We can ease your sufferings."

"You can't even do that. Let me be."

The doctor went into the drawing room and told Praskovya Fedorovna that the case was very serious and that the only resource left was opium to allay her husband's sufferings, which must be terrible.

It was true, as the doctor said, that Ivan Ilych's physical sufferings were terrible, but worse than the physical sufferings were his mental sufferings which were his chief torture.

His mental sufferings were due to the fact that that night, as he looked at Gerasim's sleepy, good-natured face with its prominent cheek-bones, the question suddenly occurred to him: "What if my whole life has been wrong?"

It occurred to him that what had appeared perfectly impossible before, namely that he had not spent his life as he should have done, might after all be true. It occurred to him that his scarcely perceptible attempts to struggle against what was considered good by the most highly placed people, those scarcely noticeable impulses which he had immediately suppressed, might have been the real thing, and all the rest false. And his professional duties and the whole arrangement of his life and of his family, and all his social and official interests, might all have been false. He tried to defend all those things to himself and suddenly felt the weakness of what he was defending. There was nothing to defend.

"But if that is so," he said to himself, "and I am leaving this life with the consciousness that I have lost all that was given me and it is impossible to rectify it—what then?" He lay on his back and began to pass his life in review in quite a new way. In the morning when he saw first his footman, then his wife, then his daughter, and then the doctor, their every word and movement confirmed to him the awful truth that had been revealed to him during the night. In them he saw himself—all that for which he had lived—and saw clearly that it was not real at all, but a terrible and huge deception which had hidden both life and death. This consciousness intensified his physical suffering tenfold. He groaned and tossed about, and pulled at his clothing which choked and stifled him. And he hated them on that account.

He was given a large dose of opium and became unconscious, but at noon his sufferings began again. He drove everybody away and tossed from side to side.

His wife came to him and said:

"Jean, my dear, do this for me. It can't do any harm and often helps. Healthy people often do it."

He opened his eyes wide.

"What? Take communion? Why? It's unnecessary! However . . . " She began to cry.

"Yes, do, my dear. I'll send for our priest. He is such a nice man."

"All right. Very well," he muttered.

When the priest came and heard his confession, Ivan Ilych was softened and seemed to feel a relief from his doubts and consequently from his sufferings, and for a moment there came a ray of hope. He again began to think of the vermiform appendix and the possibility of correcting it. He received the sacrament with tears in his eyes.

When they laid him down again afterwards he felt a moment's ease, and the hope that he might live awoke in him again. He began to think of the operation that had been suggested to him. "To live! I want to live!" he said to himself.

His wife came in to congratulate him after his communion, and when uttering the usual conventional words she added:

"You feel better, don't you?"

Without looking at her he said, "Yes."

Her dress, her figure, the expression of her face, the tone of her voice, all revealed the same thing. "This is wrong, it is not as it should be. All you have lived for and still live for is falsehood and deception, hiding life and death from you." And as soon as he admitted that thought, his hatred and his agonizing physical suffering again sprang up, and with that suffering a consciousness of the unavoidable, approaching end. And to this was added a new sensation of grinding shooting pain and a feeling of suffocation.

The expression of his face when he uttered that "Yes" was dreadful. Having uttered it, he looked her straight in the eyes, turned on his face with a rapidity extraordinary in his weak state and shouted, "Go away! Go away and leave me alone!"

From that moment the screaming began that continued for three days, and was so terrible that one could not hear it through two closed doors without horror. At the moment he answered his wife realized that he was lost, that there was no return, that the end had come, the very end, and his doubts were still unsolved and remained doubts.

"Oh! Oh! Oh!" he cried in various intonations. He had begun by screaming "I won't!" and continued screaming on the letter "O." For three whole days, during which time did not exist for him, he struggled in that black sack into which he was being thrust by an invisible, resistless force. He struggled as a man condemned to death struggles in the hands of the executioner, knowing that he cannot save himself. And every moment he felt that despite all his efforts he was drawing nearer and nearer to what terrified him. He felt that his agony was due to his being thrust into that black hole and still more to his not being able to get right into it. He was hindered from getting into it by his conviction that his life had been a good one. That very justification of his life held him fast and prevented his moving forward, and it caused him most torment of all.

Suddenly some force struck him in the chest and side, making it still harder to breathe, and he fell through the hole and there at the bottom was a light. What had happened to him was like the sensation one sometimes experiences in a railway carriage when one thinks one is going backwards while one is really going forwards and suddenly becomes aware of the real direction.

"Yes, it was not the right thing," he said to himself, "but that's no matter. It can be done. But what *is* the right thing? he asked himself, and suddenly grew quiet.

This occurred at the end of the third day, two hours before his death. Just then his schoolboy son had crept softly in and gone up to the bedside. The dying man was still screaming desperately and waving his arms. His hand fell on the boy's head, and the boy caught it, pressed it to his lips, and began to cry.

At that very moment Ivan Ilych fell through and caught sight of the light, and it was revealed to him that though his life had not been what it should have been, this could still be rectified. He asked himself, "What *is* the right thing?" and grew still, listening. Then he felt that someone was kissing his hand. He opened his eyes, looked at his son, and felt sorry for him. His wife came up to him and he glanced at her. She was gazing at him open-mouthed, with undried tears on her nose and cheek and a despairing look on her face. He felt sorry for her too.

"Yes, I am making them wretched," he thought. "They are sorry, but it will be better for them when I die." He wished to say this but had not the strength to utter it. "Besides, why speak? I must act," he thought. With a look at his wife he indicated his son and said: "Take him away . . . sorry for him . . . sorry for you too. . . . " He tried to add, "Forgive me," but said "Forego" and waved his hand, knowing that He whose understanding mattered would understand.

And suddenly it grew clear to him that what had been oppressing him and would not leave him was all dropping away at once from two sides, from ten sides, and from all sides. He was sorry for them, he must act so as not to hurt them: release them and free himself from these sufferings. "How good and how simple!" he thought. "And the pain?" he asked himself. "What has become of it? Where are you, pain?"

He turned his attention to it.

"Yes, here it is. Well, what of it? Let the pain be."

"And death . . . where is it?"

He sought his former accustomed fear of death and did not find it. "Where is it? What death?" There was no fear because there was no death.

In place of death there was light.

"So that's what it is!" he suddenly exclaimed aloud. "What joy!"

To him all this happened in a single instant, and the meaning of that instant did not change. For those present his agony continued for another two hours. Something rattled in his throat, his emaciated body twitched, then the gasping and rattle became less and less frequent.

"It is finished!" said someone near him.

He heard these words and repeated them in his soul.

"Death is finished," he said to himself. "It is no more!"

He drew in a breath, stopped in the midst of a sigh, stretched out, and died.

# 2. THE EASE OF DEATH

*For two hours after Ivan Ilych embraces death in Tolstoy's story, his body continues to thrash in its death throes. But our intuitions about dying also include a softer, easier slipping away. While his own father lay dying, Dylan Thomas wrote a poem urging him to fight with every breath, to make dying a titanic battle. The late-twentieth-century American poet Ernest Sandeen, in a tiny poem written in his eighties, plays on the title of Thomas' poem, "Do not go gentle into that good night." He suggests that the loss in old age of the strength and the will to fight hard against death may not be a bad thing, but the proper and natural rounding out of life.*

# Ernest Sandeen, "Do Not Go Gentle"

If, at the end, I seemed
to depart too willingly,
don't be distressed: I was tired,

not of having or your love,
but of being incurably old.

# 3. THE TESTIMONY OF THE DYING

*The intuitive correctness of Tolstoy's imaginative rendering of dying in* The Death of Ivan Ilych *may not be our only guide to the experience of dying, if the current popularity of "near-death experiences" is any measure. Innumerable books and articles over the last twenty years have presented accounts of people "miraculously" brought back to life after being pronounced medically dead. In this reflection, Carol Zaleski, a professor of religion at Smith College, points out the similarities and differences between these contemporary "eye-witness" accounts of life after death and those from medieval and Victorian times. She argues that cultural conditioning shapes the accounts—but argues as well that an underlying logic and consistent symbolism leaves the accounts with the possibility of being true.*

# Carol Zaleski, *The Life of the World to Come: Near-Death Experience and Christian Hope*

Near-death experience first received widespread attention in 1975 with the publication of *Life After Life* by Raymond Moody. A former philosophy professor turned psychiatrist, Moody began collecting stories of near-death experience while still in medical school. On the basis of 150 reports, Moody arrived at a description of the typical near-death experience which quickly became the standard source for portrayal of death and its aftermath in films and other popular media. Moody's book inspired several ambitious clinical studies. The subject continues to receive attention, not only in the media but also in journals of psychology and medicine, and in the publications of professional societies for near-death studies in the United States, the United Kingdom, France, Norway, Holland, and Australia.

In a 1981 Gallup survey, 15 percent of the U.S. sample reported having had a close brush with death. Of that number 34 percent claimed that the episode triggered ecstatic or visionary states of consciousness. What really accounts for the appeal of near-death testimony is not its frequency, however, but the compelling quality of the anecdotal accounts. Neither the clinical studies nor the survey results can match the impact of hearing firsthand narrative testimony from survivors who have evidently been transfigured by a close brush with death. It is tempting, therefore, to construct a master narrative, drawing upon diverse accounts, as Moody has done.

The following features recur throughout contemporary accounts:

1. Separation from the body, sometimes accompanied by a "spectator" perspective, watching the scene of crisis from a distant or elevated vantage point.

2. Journey motifs, such as drifting through darkness, outer space, a "void," or a tunnel.

3. Encounter with deceased relatives or friends, or with a godlike or angelic presence (Moody's "being of light").

4. Review of one's past deeds in the form of a panoramic visual replay of memories (the life review). In cases of sudden encounter with life-threatening danger, this life review often takes precedence over other features.

5. Immersion in light and love. Many confess that this experience is indescribable. Cognitive and affective characteristics are fused. The keynote is a profound sense of security and protection, accompanied by a sense of receiving

special messages or hidden truths. For some, this takes the form of an instantaneous, timeless, and comprehensive vision of the totality of existence.

6. Return to life, either involuntarily or by choice, to complete unfinished business on earth.

7. Transforming after-effects, such as loss of fear of death, new-found zest for everyday life, and renewed dedication to the values of empathetic love, life-long learning, and service to others. For some, these positive effects are accompanied by difficulties in adjusting to normal life.

The first reports on near-death experience in the media presented this testimony as exciting new evidence for an afterlife. In an effort to stem the tide of sensationalism, experts came forward from several quarters eager to attribute near-death experience to the mind-altering effects of drugs and anesthetics or to conditions that are part of the normal physiology of dying, such as oxygen deprivation, sensory isolation, elevated endorphin levels, and seizure activity in the brain. Near-death testimony was added to the list of targets (along with metal bending and trance channeling) for debunking attacks by members of the Committee for Scientific Investigation of Claims of the Paranormal, a group of crusading skeptics.

What both critics and researchers failed to notice was the striking evidence for the cultural shaping of near-death experience. They were unaware that what we call near-death experience today is nothing new. Stories of people who return from death, bringing back eyewitness testimony about the other world, can be found in nearly every religious tradition, and although they have many similar features, such reports invariably portray this experience in ways that conform to cultural expectations. Had the critics realized this, they no doubt would have added it to their arsenal of arguments against the veridicality of near-death experience.

What are we to make of this testimony? . . . At the risk of sounding cryptic, I would like to suggest that near-death experience is at once imaginative and real. It is a real experience mediated by the religious imagination. It is an imaginative encounter with death and a symbolic crossing of the threshold of death. Across that threshold lies the other world, which for our present purposes can be understood as the realm of the imagination, a realm in which the ideals that animate this life are encountered in their fullest, most embodied form. . . .

There are some remarkable similarities between medieval Christian return-from-death narratives and contemporary accounts of near-death experience. A template for the story would look something like this: The visionary leaves his body, looking back at it with the disinterested glance of a spectator; he is met by a luminous being who serves as his guide; he witnesses a visual replay of his past deeds, weighing them against an inner standard of right and wrong. Escorted to heavenly realms (flowery meadows, gardens, luminous cities), he is given a brief taste of the supernal delights that are the reward of the blessed. The experience is said to be indescribable—yet it is described, nonetheless, in shimmering and synaesthetic detail, as an immersion in light and love, bringing with it both ecstatic joy and intuitive knowledge. The visionary longs to remain caught up in this heavenly state, but is sent back to life. Upon returning to life, he is permanently transformed. Initially reticent, he is persuaded to tell his story for the sake of its didactic and consoling effect on others. The story is told and retold, and reshaped in the retelling, in sermons and chronicles, in scholarly treatises and across backyard fences.

There are many more similarities than I have managed to convey in this brief summary, but there are significant differences as well. Most striking, of course, is the absence from most twentieth-century near-death accounts of postmortem punishment: no hell, no purgatory, no chastening torments or telltale agonies at the moment of death. The life review, when it occurs, is a reassuring experience, modeled on contemporary methods of education and psychotherapy. The guide figure is often a family member or a generic spiritual presence, and is always friendly and comforting. In the medieval accounts the guide is usually a guardian angel or patron saint, who for the sake of the visionary's eventual salvation is not above dangling his charge over the pit of hell. The possibility for loss is genuine in the medieval accounts—if one botches the second chance, eternal damnation is the likely result. Today it seems that there is scarcely any possibility for loss. Life and afterlife flow together as an unending stream of fresh opportunities for personal growth.

What of the transforming effects of the near-death experience? Today they take the form of freedom from everyday worries and from fear of death, poignant appreciation for the ordinary moments of life, and passionate dedication to the values of love, learning, and service. The social expression of these values varies greatly. Medieval accounts have a more penitential theme, and expect the visionary to express his transformed state of mind in a sanctioned institutional form, for example, as a pilgrim or monk.

The similarities suggest that there are some enduring—perhaps even universal features of near-death experience. The differences make it clear, however, that near-death experiences, and the literature that describes them, are profoundly shaped by cultural expectations. The researchers have been naive about this point, claiming that the lack of what they call "traditional" features (St. Peter at the gate or demons with pitchforks) is a sign of freedom from mythology.

At this point, we totter perilously close to the edge of dismissing near-death testimony as "nothing but" a projection of cultural values, wishes, and norms. Only a lively appreciation for the revelatory potential of the religious imagination can keep us from falling over that edge into the fold of the skeptics and debunkers. . . . A near-death experiencer is certain that he was dead; the experts say no. I say yes, in a way; it was a visionary encounter with death. The visionary "met his death" (note that this phrase retains a vestige of the image of death as a person). In that symbolic encounter, the visionary entered the other world—that is, the domain of the imagination, the inner world turned inside out and projected on the stage of imagination. On this stage the drama of life and death, judgment and redemption, is acted out. . . .

A great deal depends upon how one understands symbol. . . . No matter how genuine, the symbol can never become completely transparent to the reality it represents. We cannot know what awaits us after death, but we can legitimately believe all that our tradition teaches and our experience suggests. We believe all this under correction; and—if we love a good surprise—we look forward to the correction.

The truth about eschatology is itself eschatological. Now we see in an enigma darkly, in the mirror of our culture. Only "then," when the veil is lifted, shall we see face to face. Now we must test the soundness of our images and symbols by practicing the traditional and modern arts of discernment, guided by both dogma and experience. Only then shall we know as we are known. . . .

I have mentioned that one of the striking features of contemporary near-death literature is the absence of hell, purgatory, and postmortem punishment. This is partly attributable to the liberal proclivities of the researchers; markedly different results are reported by conservative evangelical Christians who have studied near-death phenomena. But if notions of sin and punishment are suppressed in the popular accounts, there is, nonetheless, plenty of evidence for the persistence—though in camouflaged form—of the notion of judgment. The form in which the motif of judgment persists is the "life review."

Although not an inevitable feature of near-death reports, the life review episode occurs in a wide variety of narratives. Even before the term "near-death experience" was coined, the idea that a drowning man sees his life pass before him had been planted in the popular imagination (where it quickly acquired the status of proverbial wisdom) by its treatment in several widely read nineteenth-century English and American memoirs and medical essays. . . . Among the common features are the sense of the self as a spectator, the attitude of serene detachment, the comprehensiveness and simultaneity of the visual replay of memories, and the implication that the life review constitutes a final summation and judgment of one's character and history. . . .

If death sets the seal on one's identity, then the life review is the narrative act by which one becomes a whole person, a person whose life story is complete. The panoramic and instantaneous character of this review is particularly significant, for it suggests that one is no longer, as Augustine lamented, torn between time past and time to come. All times have been gathered together, all past experience witnessed and offered up in a comprehensive and simultaneous thought that distantly mirrors the comprehensive and simultaneous wholeness of divine thought. This is precisely the kind of memory to which Augustine appealed when he set out to make his *confessio* or sacrificial offering of his life story to God and to the reader.

So far, I have suggested that the life review is a completing the life story and a gathering together of one's memories to make of oneself a whole offering, a perfect holocaust, at the moment of the imagined encounter with death. In what sense, though, is the life review analogous to postmortem judgment? It corresponds to one of the most common symbolic modalities for postmortem judgment: the encounter with one's deeds in externalized form, for example, recorded in a book, weighed upon a scale, reflected in a mirror, or dramatized, as in a psychomachy, by a pitched battle of virtues against vices.

The third-century apocalypse known to the West as the *Vis Pauli* depicts the soul's exit from the body as a critical moment in which the entire history of one's actions and intentions is displayed in visible form: first, as a written record of deeds and then as a confrontation with the souls whom one has injured in life. In one medieval version of this text an angel asks Paul, "Have you believed and known, that whatever each one of you has done, he sees in the hour of his need?" The scriptural basis for this comes from I Corinthians 3, where Paul says that "every man's work shall be made manifest" on the day of the Lord, and shall be tested by fire. What is striking in this medieval version of the apocalypse of Paul is that the encounter with deeds has been transferred from the day of the Lord to the time of death.

Similarly, in the *Dialogues* of Gregory the Great, those who die and return report seeing their good and evil works made manifest in the form of symbolic buildings, personifications, and dramatic encounters. Gregory interprets the other world entirely as a symbolic landscape, in which the visionary confronts his own soul and thus brings judgment upon himself.

Two developments in the medieval Christian motif of encounter with deeds are especially worthy of note:

1. The transfer of judgment from the Last Day to the interim period and from the interim period to the deathbed. Judgment thereby becomes an expected part of the near-death experience, as well as an anticipated scenario for end times. The redundancy was apparently not considered a problem.

2. A change in the character of this encounter, from an impartial modality of judgment to a contest between mercy and judgment. In several medieval

return-from-death accounts, visionaries read the record of their sins only to discover that a few tears, looked upon kindly by the Blessed Virgin or the Lord, will be enough to erase the record. In the fifteenth-century illustrated *artes moriendi* (guidebooks on the art, or craft, of dying), the record of deeds (looking for all the world like one of those old-fashioned computer punch cards that must not be bent, spindled, or mutilated) is in the hands of the demons, who wave it in the dying man's face in order to tempt him to despair. The angels make use of the same record only when they need to provide countervailing force against the temptation to vainglory or overconfidence. More often than not, the role of the angelic party is to try to destroy the damaging evidence. Thus the encounter with deeds becomes an object lesson in the need to take refuge in divine mercy and, above all, in the intercession of the Blessed Virgin and the saints.

If we turn to the vestiges of this motif as they occur in contemporary near-death testimony, these two points have striking relevance, even if we accept the view that our culture is post-Christian. First, the transfer of judgment to the deathbed stuck; the emphasis is on the individual as he or she meets death. This emphasis on the individual heightens anxiety and therefore increases the need for consoling reassurances. Second, the encounter with deeds is, for the reason I just mentioned, an occasion to be reassured about one's worth. The only reason the appeal for mercy is not heard so clearly today is that the encounter with deeds is from start to finish a reassuring and therapeutic exercise. There is no sense of being judged by an external being; rather, the emphasis is on self-evaluation, learning, and growth.

The following example is typical:

> And into this great peace that I had become there came the life of Phyllis parading past my view. . . . The reliving included not only the deeds committed by Phyllis since her birth . . . but also a reliving of every thought ever thought and every word ever spoken PLUS the effect of every thought, word and deed upon everyone and anyone who had ever come within her sphere of influence whether she actually knew them or not PLUS the effect of her every thought, word and deed upon the weather, the soil, plants and animals, the water, everything else. . . . I never before realized that we were responsible and accountable for EVERY SINGLE THING WE DID. That was overwhelming!
>
> It was me judging me, not some heavenly St. Peter. And my judgment was critical and stern. I was not satisfied with many, many things Phyllis had done, said or thought. There was a feeling of sadness and failure, yet a growing feeling of joy when the reaction came that Phyllis had always done SOMETHING. . . . She tried. Much of what she did was constructive and positive. She learned and grew in her learning. This was satisfying. Phyllis was okay.

This much we can say for the judgment scenarios of contemporary near-death testimony: although they may be excessively privatistic and optimistic, they at least avoid the unbecoming trait of taking satisfaction in contemplating the doom of others. If we step back and take the long view of the history of judgment motifs in Christian eschatology, we can see that modulated by the many—even redundant—media of forgiveness and reconciliation, the anticipation of judgment is part of what gives life meaning and direction. It completes the life story and thus provides the necessary prelude to the consummation of our common life.

# 4. CHOOSING SUICIDE

*Though we cannot always choose to live, it seems we have the power to control how we die: following the model of the Roman Stoics, some writers—including the essayist Montaigne, the philosopher David Hume, and the American newspaperman Ambrose Bierce—have recommended suicide as a courageous answer to dishonor and pain. Perhaps the most important twentieth-century essay to put the moral and philosophical case against suicide is Albert Camus'* The Myth of Sisyphus. *But the British literary critic A. Alvarez, in the prologue to his 1971 study of suicide,* The Savage God, *puts what may be an even more compelling case. Describing the suicide of his friend, the American poet Sylvia Plath (1932–63), he seeks both to understand and to forgive—and seeks beyond them both for a judgment of the fillip of interest Plath's suicide gave to her poetry. "Despair," Alvarez declares later in his book, "seeks its own environment as surely as water finds its own level." Plath's suicidal despair may have been a brilliant one, for she was brilliant. But it remained only despair.*

# A. Alvarez, *The Savage God*

It was an unspeakable winter, the worst, they said, in a hundred and fifty years. The snow began just after Christmas and would not let up. By New Year the whole country had ground to a halt. The trains froze on the tracks, the abandoned trucks froze on the roads. The power stations, overloaded by million upon pathetic million of hopeless electric fires, broke down continually; not that the fires mattered, since the electricians were mostly out on strike. Water pipes froze solid; for a bath you had to scheme and cajole those rare friends with centrally-heated houses, who became rarer and less friendly as the weeks dragged on. Doing the dishes became a major operation. The gastric rumble of water in outdated plumbing was sweeter than the sound of mandolins. Weight for weight, plumbers were as expensive as smoked salmon and harder to find. The gas failed and Sunday roasts were raw. The lights failed and candles, of course, were unobtainable. Nerves failed and marriages crumbled. Finally, the heart failed. It seemed the cold would never end. Nag, nag, nag.

In December the *Observer* had published a long-uncollected poem by Sylvia called "Event"; in mid-January they published another, "Winter Trace." Sylvia wrote me a note about it, adding that maybe we should take our children to the zoo and she would show me "the nude verdigris of the condor." But she no longer dropped into my studio with poems. Later that month I met a literary editor of one of the big weeklies. He asked me if I had seen Sylvia recently.

"No. Why?"

"I was just wondering. She sent us some poems. Very strange."

"Did you like them?"

"No," he replied, "too extreme for my taste. I sent them all back. But she sounds in a bad state. I think she needs help."

Her doctor, a sensitive, overworked man, thought the same. He prescribed sedatives and arranged for her to see a psychotherapist. Having been bitten once by American psychiatry, she hesitated for some time before writing for an appointment. But her depression did not lift and finally the letter was sent. It did no good. Either her letter or that of the therapist arranging a consultation went astray; apparently the postman delivered it to the wrong address. The therapist's reply arrived a day or two after she died. This was one of several links in the chain of accidents, coincidences and mistakes that ended in her death.

I am convinced by what I know of the facts that this time she did not intend to die. Her suicide attempt ten years before had been, in every sense, deadly serious. She had carefully disguised the theft of the sleeping pills, left a misleading note to cover her tracks, and hidden herself in the darkest, most unused corner of a cellar, rearranging behind her the old firelogs she had disturbed, burying herself away like a skeleton in the nethermost family closet. Then she had swallowed a bottle of fifty sleeping pills. She was found late and by accident, and survived only by a miracle. The flow of life in her was too strong even for the violence she had done it. This, anyway, is her description of the act in *The Bell Jar;* there is no reason to believe it false. So she had learned the hard way the odds against successful suicide; she had learned that despair must be counterpoised by an almost obsessional attention to detail and disguise.

By these lights she seemed, in her last attempt, to be taking care not to succeed. But this time everything conspired to destroy her. An employment agency had found her an au pair girl to help with the children and housework while Sylvia got on with her writing. The girl, an Australian, was due to arrive at nine o'clock on the morning of Monday, February 11. Meanwhile, a recurrent trouble, her sinuses were bad; the pipes in her newly converted flat froze solid; there was still no telephone, and no word from the psychotherapist; the weather continued monstrous. Illness, loneliness, depression and cold, combined with the demands of two small children were too much for her. So when the weekend came she went off with the babies to stay with friends in another part of London. The plan was, I think, that she would leave early enough on Monday morning to be back in time to welcome the Australian girl. Instead, she decided to go back on Sunday. The friends were against it but she was insistent, made a great show of her old competence and seemed more cheerful than she had done for some time. So they let her go. About eleven o'clock that night she knocked on the door of the elderly painter who lived below her, asking to borrow some stamps. But she lingered in the doorway, drawing out the conversation until he told her that he got up well before nine in the morning. Then she said good night and went back upstairs.

God knows what kind of a sleepless night she spent or if she wrote any poetry. Certainly, within the last few days of her life she wrote one of her most beautiful poems, "Edge," which is specifically about the act she was about to perform. . . . It is a poem of great peace and resignation, utterly without self-pity. Even with a subject so appallingly close she remains an artist, absorbed in the practical task of letting each image develop a full, still life of its own. That she is writing about her own death is almost irrelevant. There is another poem, "Words," also very late, which is about the way language remains and echoes long after the turmoil of life has passed; like "Edge," it has the same translucent calm. If these were among the last things she wrote, I think she must in the end have accepted the logic of the life she had been leading and come to terms with its terrible necessities.

Around six o'clock that morning, she went up to the children's room and left a plate of bread and butter and two mugs of milk, in case they should wake hungry before the au pair girl arrived. Then she went back down to the kitchen, sealed the door and window as best she could with towels, opened the oven, laid her head in it and turned on the gas.

The Australian girl arrived punctually at nine o'clock. She rang and knocked a long time but could get no answer. So she went off to search for a telephone booth in order to phone the agency and make sure she had the right address. Sylvia's name, incidentally, was not on either of the doorbells. Had everything been normal, the neighbor below would have been up by then; even if he had overslept, the girl's knocking should have aroused him. But as it happened, the neighbor was very deaf and slept without his hearing aid. More important, his bedroom was immediately below Sylvia's kitchen. The gas seeped down and knocked him out cold. So he slept on through all the noise. The girl returned and tried again, still without success. Again she went off to telephone the agency and ask what to do; they told her to go back. It was now about eleven o'clock. This time she was lucky: some builders had arrived to work in the frozen-up house, and they let her in. When she knocked on Sylvia's door there was no answer and the smell of gas was overpowering. The builders forced the lock and found Sylvia sprawled in the kitchen. She was still warm. She had left a note saying "Please call Dr. _____" and giving his telephone number. But it was too late.

Had everything worked out as it should—had the gas not drugged the man downstairs, preventing him from opening the front door to the au pair girl—there is little doubt she would have been saved. I think she wanted to be; why else leave her doctor's telephone number? This time, unlike the occasion ten years before, there was too much holding her to life. Above all, there were the children: she was too passionate a mother to want to lose them or them to lose her. There were also the extraordinary creative powers she now unequivocally knew she possessed: the poems came daily, unbidden and unstoppable, and she was again working on a novel about which, at last, she had no reservations.

Why, then, did she kill herself? In part, I suppose, it was "a cry for help" which fatally misfired. But it was also a last desperate attempt to exorcise the death she had summed up in her poems. I have already suggested that perhaps she had begun to write obsessively about death for two reasons. First, when she and her husband separated, however mutual the arrangement, she again went through the same piercing grief and bereavement she had felt as a child when her father, by his death, seemed to abandon her. Second, I believe she thought her car crash the previous summer had set her free; she had paid her dues, qualified as a survivor and could now write about it. But as I have written elsewhere, for the artist himself art is not necessarily therapeutic; he is not automatically relieved of his fantasies by expressing them. Instead, by some perverse logic of creation, the act of formal expression may simply make the dredged-up material more readily available to him. The result of handling it in his work may well be that he finds himself living it out. For the artist, in short, nature often imitates art. Or, to change the cliche, when an artist holds up a mirror to nature he finds out who and what he is; but the knowledge may change him irredeemably so that he becomes that image.

I think Sylvia, in one way or another, sensed this. In an introductory note she wrote to "Daddy" for the BBC she said of the poem's narrator, "She has to act out the awful little allegory once over before she is free of it." The allegory in question was, as she saw it, the struggle in her between a fantasy Nazi father and a Jewish mother. But perhaps it was also a fantasy of containing in herself her own dead father, like a woman possessed by a demon (in the poem she actually calls him a vampire). In order for her to be free of him, he had to be released like a genie from a bottle. And this is precisely what the poems did: they bodied forth the death within her. But they also did so in an intensely living and creative way. The more she wrote about death, the stronger and more fertile her imaginative world became. And this gave her everything to live for.

I suspect that in the end she wanted to have done with the theme once and for all. But the only way she could find was "to act out the awful little allegory once over." She had always been a bit of a gambler, used to taking risks. The authority of her poetry was in part due to her brave persistence in following the thread of her inspiration right down to the Minotaur's lair. And this psychic courage had its parallel in her physical arrogance and carelessness. Risks didn't frighten her; on the contrary, she found them stimulating. Freud has written: "Life loses in interest, when the highest stake in the game of living, life itself, may not be risked." Finally, Sylvia took that risk. She gambled for the last time, having worked out that the odds were in her favor, but perhaps, in her depression, not much caring whether she won or lost. Her calculations went wrong and she lost.

It was a mistake, then, and out of it a whole myth has grown. I don't think she would have found it much to her taste, since it is a myth of the poet as a sacrificial victim, offering herself up for the sake of her art, having been dragged by the Muses to that final altar through every kind of distress. In these terms, her suicide becomes the whole point of the story, the act which validates her poems, gives them their interest and proves her seriousness. So people are drawn to her work in much the same spirit as *Time* magazine featured her at length: not for the poetry but for the gossipy, extra-literary "human interest." Yet just as the suicide adds nothing at all to the poetry, so the myth of Sylvia as a passive victim is a total perversion of the woman she was. It misses altogether her liveliness, her intellectual appetite and harsh wit, her great imaginative resourcefulness and vehemence of feeling, her control. Above all, it misses the courage with which she was able to turn disaster into art. The pity is not that there is a myth of Sylvia Plath, but that the myth is not simply that of an enormously gifted poet whose death came carelessly, by mistake and too soon.

I used to think of her brightness as a facade, as though she were able, in a rather schizoid way, to turn her back on her suffering for the sake of appearance, and pretend it didn't exist. But maybe she was also able to keep her unhappiness in check because she could write about it, because she knew she was salvaging from all those horrors something rather marvelous. The end came when she felt she could stand the subject no longer. She had written it out and was ready for something new. . . . The only method of stopping it she could see, her vision by then blinkered by depression and illness, was that last gamble. So having, as she thought, arranged to be saved, she lay down in front of the gas oven almost hopefully, almost with relief, as though she were saying, "Perhaps this will set me free."

On Friday, February 15, there was an inquest in the drab, damp coroner's court behind Camden Town: muttered evidence, long silences, the Australian girl in tears. Earlier that morning I had gone with Ted to the undertaker's in Mornington Crescent. The coffin was at the far end of a bare, draped room. She lay stiffly, a ludicrous ruff at her neck. Only her face showed. It was gray and slightly transparent, like wax. I had never before seen a dead person and I hardly recognized her; her features seemed too thin and sharp. The room smelled of apples, faint, sweet but somehow unclean, as though the apples were beginning to rot. I was glad to get out into the cold and noise of the dingy streets. It seemed impossible that she was dead.

Even now I find it hard to believe. There was too much life in her long, flat, strongly boned body, and her longish face with its fine brown eyes, shrewd and full of feeling. She was practical and candid, passionate and compassionate. I believe she was a genius. I sometimes catch myself childishly thinking I'll run into her walking Primrose Hill or the Heath, and we'll pick up the conversation where we left off. But perhaps that is because her poems still speak so distinctly in her accents: quick, sardonic, unpredictable, effortlessly inventive, a bit angry, and always utterly her own.

# 5. CHOOSING TO LIVE

*In the pain suffered by Tolstoy's Ivan Ilych, as well as in the arguments for allowing or even praising suicide, there seem to be reasons for euthanasia—for leaping over dying, straight to death. In Holland, euthanasia has become a pervasive cultural institution, and there are those—like the Hemlock Society—who hope it will become that in the United States. This hope for a dyingless death without pain or suffering may mark a cultural shift of enormous proportions, when contrasted with John Donne's claim that "affliction is a treasure and scarce any man hath enough of it." But it is often coupled with a very old-fashioned claim that the sufferers hope to spare others the burden of caring for them. In this brief 1993 essay, Gilbert Meilaender, a professor of religion at Valparaiso University, faces the question of being a burden to one's family and suggests that we have reasons and even responsibilities not to bypass our dying.*

# Gilbert Meilaender, "I Want to Burden My Loved Ones"

Recently I was a speaker and panel member at a small educational workshop on "advance directives" sponsored by the ethics committee of our local hospital. The workshop was an opportunity to provide information about, and discuss the relative merits of, living wills and durable powers of attorney as different ways of trying to deal in advance with medical decisions that might have to be made for us after we have become incompetent. This is not the first such workshop for me, and I suppose it may not be the last. And I was struck, as I have been before, with the recurrence of a certain theme.

Many people come to such a workshop already quite knowledgeable about the topic to be discussed. They come less for information than for the opportunity to talk. Some earnestly desire the chance to converse about a troubling issue; a few just want to express themselves. In either case, however, it is remarkable how often they may say something like the following: "I'm afraid that if my children have to make decisions about my care, they won't be able to handle the pressure. They'll just argue with each other, and they'll feel guilty, wondering whether they're really doing what I would want. I don't want to be a burden to them, and I will do whatever I can in advance to see that I'm not." And after someone has spoken words to this effect, there will be a chorus of assent from the people who, evidently, share the speaker's view.

Now, of course, we can in many ways understand and appreciate such a perspective. None of us wishes to imagine his children arguing together about who really knows best how he should be treated (or not treated). We hate to think that our children's last thoughts of us would be interwoven with anger at each other, guilt for their uncertainty about how best to care for us, or even (perhaps) a secret wish that we'd get on with the dying and relieve them of this burden.

Nonetheless, as the workshop wore on, I found myself giving it only a part of my attention, because I couldn't help musing on this recurring theme. Understandable as it surely is in many respects, there is, I am convinced, something wrong with it. I don't know how to make the point other than a little too crassly—other than by saying that I want to be a burden to my loved ones. But, rightly understood, I think I do. The first thought that occurred to me in my musings was not, I admit, the noblest: I have sweated in the hot sun teaching four children to catch and hit a ball, to swing a tennis racket and shoot a free throw. I have built blocks and played games I detest with and for my children. I have watched countless basketball games made up largely of bad passes, traveling violations, and shots that missed both rim and backboard. I have sat through years of piano recitals, band concerts, school programs—often on very busy nights or very hot, humid evenings in late spring. I have stood in a steamy bathroom in the middle of the night with the hot shower running, trying to help a child with croup breathe more easily. I have run beside a bicycle, ready to catch a child who might fall while learning to ride. (This is, by the way, very hard!) I have spent hours finding perfectly decent (cheap) clothing in stores, only to have these choices rejected as somehow not exactly what we had in mind. I have used evenings to type in final form long stories—longer by far than necessary—that my children have written in response to school assignments. I have had to fight for the right to eat at Burger King rather than McDonald's. Why should I not be a bit of a burden to these children in my dying?

This was not, I have already granted, the noblest thought, but it was the first. And, of course, it overlooks a great deal—above all, that I have taken great joy in these children and have not really resented much in the litany of burdens recited above. But still, there is here a serious point to be considered. Is this not in large measure what it means to belong to a family: to burden each other—and to find, almost miraculously that others are willing, even happy, to carry such burdens? Families would not have the significance they do for us if they did not, in fact, give us a claim upon each other. At least in this sphere of life we do not come together as autonomous individuals freely contracting with each other. We simply find ourselves thrown together and asked to share the burdens of life while learning to care for each other. We may often resent such claims on our time and energies. We did not, after all, consent to them. (Or, at least, if we want to speak of consent, it will have to be something like that old staple of social-contract theorists, tacit consent.)

It is, therefore, understandable that we sometimes chafe under these burdens. If, however, we also go on to reject them, we cease to live in the kind of moral community that deserves to be called a family. Here more than in any other sphere of life we are presented with unwanted and unexpected interruptions to our plans and projects. I do not like such interruptions any more than the next person; indeed, a little less, I rather suspect. But it is still true that morality consists in large part in learning to deal with the unwanted and unexpected interruptions to our plans. I have tried, subject to my limits and weaknesses, to teach that lesson to my children. Perhaps I will teach it best when I am a burden to them in my dying. This was my first thought. It led to a second.

Perhaps it is a good thing, lest we be tempted to injustice, that the dying burden the living. Some years ago Robert Burt wrote a book about medical decision-making for incompetent patients. The book's title was *Taking Care of*

*Strangers.* Burt's point, which carried a double entendre, was essentially this: Patients who are unable to make decisions for themselves are often in a state (e.g., severely demented, comatose) in which they become strangers to us. They make us uneasy and we react with ambivalence. And to say, "I'll take care of him" about such a patient may be a statement freighted with ambivalence. Burt worries that, no matter how devoted our care, our uneasiness with a loved one who has become a stranger to us may prompt us to do less than we ought to sustain his life. (Nor, should we note, are physicians immune to such uneasiness.) It is, therefore, essential that we structure the medical decision-making situation in such a way that conversation is forced among the doctor, the medical caregivers, the patient's family, and perhaps still others, such as pastor, priest, or rabbi. Advance directives, designed to eliminate the need for such extended conversation—lest it should burden loved ones—are, from this perspective, somewhat problematic. They may not force us to deal with our own ambivalence in "taking care of" a loved one who is now a burdensome stranger.

This does not mean that advance directives are entirely a bad idea. It does suggest, however, that a durable power of attorney for medical care—in which we simply name a proxy to make decisions in the event of our incompetence—is better than a living will in which we attempt to state the kinds of treatment we would or would not desire under a variety of medical circumstances. At this point in my life, for example, I would surely turn over to my wife my power of attorney. In doing so I simply announce to medical caregivers: "Here is the person with whom you must converse when the day comes that you cannot talk with me about my medical care." I myself do not particularly like the recently fashionable attempts to combine the two forms of advance directives by naming a proxy and giving that proxy as much detail as possible about what we would want done. That move—though, again, it will be seen as an attempt to avoid burdening the loved one who must make such decisions—may not, in any case, accomplish our aim. What it commits us to is an endless, futile search to determine what a now-incompetent person would wish. Still more important, it is one last-ditch attempt to bypass the interdependence of human life, by which we simply do and should constitute a burden to those who love us.

I hope, therefore, that I will have the good sense to empower my wife, while she is able, to make such decisions for me—though I know full well that we do not always agree about what is the best care in end-of-life circumstances. That disagreement doesn't bother me at all. As long as she avoids the futile question, "What would he have wanted?" and contents herself with the (difficult enough) question, "What is best for him now?" I will have no quarrel with her. Moreover, this approach is, I think, less likely to encourage her to make the moral mistake of asking, "Is his life a benefit to him (i.e., a life worth living)?" and more likely to encourage her to ask, "What can we do to benefit the life he still has?" No doubt this will be a burden to her. No doubt she will bear the burden better than I would. No doubt it will be only the last in a long history of burdens she has borne for me. But then, mystery and continuous miracle that it is, she loves me. And because she does, I must of course be a burden to her.

# 6. HASTENING DEATH

*The idea that we can control our dying is not new: the ancient Stoics recommended suicide as a device with which to take charge of death. But in recent years there has emerged a new interest in physician-aided suicide and the killing of people who are suffering. In this letter that might have come from a Roman administrator posted in Palestine, Jeffrey Ford—an assistant professor of history at Northwestern College in Orange City, Iowa—shows the classical roots of the idea of mercy killing and, in his surprise ending, its opposition to the Christian view of a death that has meaning and a suffering that can be redemptive.*

# Jeffrey E. Ford, "Mercy Killing at Golgotha"

L. Annaeus Seneca, Greetings from your uncle Claudius in Palestine.

Whoever thought it best to extend the empire to this gods-forsaken corner of land ought to be put to the sword. There is nothing here except zealotry and fanaticism, political and religious. The population is in perpetual revolt and it takes a legion just to hold Jerusalem. The Jews neither honor the gods nor delight in the civilities of life. Their food is plain, their language coarse, their women rude. Even a Deputy Governor suffers in this desert. When the people are not driving him mad, the heat is.

I write, however, not to complain of my tribulations. I gladly endure them for the sake of Rome—and besides, soon enough, I return home, my service accomplished, my future secured. Rather, I have a story I want to tell you, perhaps to explain to you something more of my philosophy of life, continuing discussions you and I have had before.

Yesterday we executed a rebel. The man was in his early thirties, about your age. He was Jewish, and was put to death by popular acclaim. As is the custom, he was scourged before being forced to drag his cross to the place of execution, where he was nailed and left to die. The man was rather weak and expired quickly, as far as these things go.

Of course, no one dies immediately when crucified. This death is as painful a way to die as any I have seen. Spikes are driven through the criminal's wrists and ankles, his torn flesh almost immediately beginning to swell. As the man's own weight pulls at his wounds, the slightest movement, even breathing, becomes agonizing. The man slowly loses strength, painfully shifting and propping his body to take in every possible breath. Very few give themselves over to death, but scream and shriek until they lose the power to protest their pain. Finally, in the criminal's chest—crushed as though piled under heavy stones—his heart bursts and he dies in one last moment of agony.

You have seen crucified slaves and know what I am talking about. You also know what I believe about crucifixion. I have no objection to capital punishment. It alone avenges capital crimes and ensures public order. Without the sword, our empire would collapse in a day. Yet I cannot bring myself to enjoy crucifixion as so many of the legionnaires do. This form of execution causes not only men in the ranks but even centurions and tribunes to adopt an excessively harsh view of life, sometimes laughing and joking a few feet away from a bloody cross—like mere barbarians. Yesterday, I saw several soldiers gambling for the cloak of the condemned criminal, making sport of his last possession, stained with his own blood. The sight cost me a night's sleep, and not for the first time.

Still, no matter what the legions do to subject peoples and condemned criminals, I am convinced that it is my duty to live without any differentiating among men. You know my thoughts. I believe all men to be equal before nature, and thus acts just or merciful for Romans are also just or merciful for Jews. Discovering the standard by which to judge all human beings seems to me, in fact, to be the very goal of philosophy. I do not treat Jews and Romans differently, at least as far as ethics is concerned.

And that is why I intervened on behalf of the condemned rebel yesterday. As you know, it is accepted in Rome that a man should be free to commit suicide if he is about to be overwhelmed by calamity, persecution, or suffering. There is not a family in Rome that has not stood by while a loved one opened his veins and bled to death in a tub of warm water. It is my belief that this ethically justifiable mercy should be extended to Jews and barbarians as well, without favoritism or partiality. Such is the rule of nature and philosophy.

Therefore, I treated the crucified Jew as I would have a Roman. When he was taken to his place of execution, suffering agonizing pain after being nailed to his cross, I asked the attending centurion for permission to alleviate the man's pain. Because the officer owed me a favor, he granted my request and allowed me to provide a humane death to the suffering Jew. I filled a bowl with wine, gall, and arsenic, then offered it to the condemned man. I could tell by his eyes that he understood the nature of my offer. He drank of the wine. A few minutes later the man was dead, spared the pointless and extended agony of crucifixion. Pilate had his corpse and the criminal his release from hours of excruciating suffering, pain devoid of value and purpose.

Yet something bothers me when I think about the scene. I offered the poisoned wine to the criminal just as he was giving his friends and family final advice and instructions. Because he drank of my wine as soon as it was offered, he was unable to speak any longer, an effect that he evidently had not expected. I have never seen such despair as I saw when the man realized that he could no longer talk. Though he had uttered only a few anguished words beforehand, after drinking the wine he could no longer speak at all. His throat was constricted too tightly for him to utter a single word as he hung on his cross for a minute or two, gasping and trembling, and trying to speak. Finally, he cried out with all of the strength that remained in his body, "It is not finished!" Then he died.

I do not know what he wanted to say or to accomplish hanging from a cross, but he apparently believed that something had been missed—and it was my fault. Just as he died, he looked in my direction, searing my soul with a look of furious indignation—as though I were the one who had condemned him to a pointless death on a cross, as though I were his betrayer. This criminal, who had made a point of forgiving his executioners minutes earlier, looked upon me with an anger that was inhuman. I saved the man from a death of hours, perhaps days, yet he looked at me in hatred.

It is not hard to imagine why he would have despised Pilate, the military guard, or the taunting mob, but he hated me—the one Roman in the whole empire who pitied his suffering. Perhaps he did have a few things to say to his family, but what great thing could he accomplish on a cross? Unless he had the power to tear himself from his tree, it was certain that he would die a terrible and painful death. And even fools admit that nothing good can be accomplished by needless suffering and useless pain.

I saved the man pain and humiliation, and I saved his family from the extension of their sorrow. Does a man stricken with a tumor earn virtue by living on in pain? Does a woman consumed by plague accomplish anything by allowing her death to linger for a few days more? Are families honored by sharing in the agonies of death?

A reasonable man would have thanked me for my mercy, for giving to a condemned Jew the same privilege enjoyed by a Roman Senator. And the whole world would agree. Only this one damnable Jew seems to have thought that he had something to gain by suffering torture and humiliation for a few hours more. Perhaps you can see why I loathe living in this desert. I must go now. There is work to be done. Pilate has just sent word that another crucifixion has been decreed—this time a miracle-working prophet found guilty of blasphemy and sedition. I suspect even Rome will feel tremors from this execution, since the man has a large following of fanatical disciples, some of whom are armed.

Perhaps I can calm the outcry at his death by alleviating his suffering as I did the other condemned rebel. An act of mercy may do some good. And since the man is something of a philosopher himself, though in a rude and coarse manner, perhaps he will appreciate my gesture better than did the other Jew, especially since he has often expressed a disdain for death—provoking Roman and Jew alike with his teachings and antics. In any case, it will be interesting to see if this Jewish rabbi can die with the dignity of a Roman philosopher.

Our lives are completed in our deaths, Seneca. That is why I will preach the virtue of a noble death to the end of my own days and hope that you will do the same. No man can live well who is not prepared to die well. So always live and die as a Roman. And remember, too, to sacrifice to the gods whenever you worship at the temples. The gods must be placated if our house is to continue to rise. And whatever their reasons are, they insist upon blood sacrifice. So offer a ram for me, since it is nearly impossible to perform the proper sacrifices while living among the Jews. I hope to see you in Rome by winter.

Your uncle, Claudius Letum Dignitate

# 7. HOLDING STILL FOR DEATH

*On May 24, 1996, a group of Islamic terrorists announced that they had "slit the throats" of seven French Trappist monks whom they had kidnapped from the monastery of Titherine in Algeria and held as hostages for two months. Prior to the kidnapping, the superior of the monastery, Father Christian de Chergé, had left with his family this testament "to be opened in the event of my death." Like heroic death in war, martyrdom is distinguishable from suicide in part because of its obedience to something higher, but in greater part because it does not seek death as an escape from the world. It seeks, rather, to make death—when death comes—an event with consequence for the universe it knows will continue after death.*

# Christian de Chergé, "Last Testament"

If it should happen one day—and it could be today—that I become a victim of the terrorism which now seems ready to encompass all the foreigners living in Algeria, I would like my community, my church, my family, to remember that my life was given to God and to this country. I ask them to accept that the One Master of all life was not a stranger to this brutal departure. I ask them to pray for me: for how could I be found worthy of such an offering? I ask them to be able to associate such a death with the many other deaths that were just as violent, but forgotten through indifference and anonymity.

My life has no more value than any other. Nor any less value. In any case, it has not the innocence of childhood. I have lived long enough to know that I share in the evil which seems, alas, to prevail in the world, even in that which would strike me blindly. I should like, when the time comes, to have a clear space which would allow me to beg forgiveness of God and of all my fellow human beings, and at the same time to forgive with all my heart the one who would strike me down.

I could not desire such a death. It seems to me important to state this. I do not see, in fact, how I could rejoice if this people I love were to be accused indiscriminately of my murder. It would be to pay too dearly for what will, perhaps, be called "the grace of martyrdom," to owe it to an Algerian, whoever he may be, especially if he says he is acting in fidelity to what he believes to be Islam. I know the scorn with which Algerians as a whole can be regarded. I know also the caricature of Islam which a certain kind of Islamism encourages. It is too easy to give oneself a good conscience by identifying this religious way with the fundamentalist ideologies of the extremists. For me, Algeria and Islam are something different; they are a body and a soul. I have proclaimed this often enough, I believe, in the sure knowledge of what I have received in Algeria, in the respect of believing Muslims—finding there so often that true strand of the Gospel I learned at my mother's knee, my very first church.

My death, clearly, will appear to justify those who hastily judged me naive or idealistic: "Let him tell us now what he thinks of it!" But these people must realize that my most avid curiosity will then be satisfied. This is what I shall be able to do, if God wills—immerse my gaze in that of the Father, to contemplate with him his children of Islam just as he sees them, all shining with the glory of Christ, the fruit of his Passion, filled with the Gift of the Spirit, whose secret joy will always be to establish communion and to refashion the likeness, delighting in the differences.

For this life given up, totally mine and totally theirs, I thank God who seems to have wished it entirely for the sake of that joy in everything and in spite of everything. In this "thank you," which is said for everything in my life from now on, I certainly include you, friends of yesterday and today, and you my friends of this place, along with my mother and father, my brothers and sisters and their families—the hundredfold granted as was promised!

And you also, the friend of my final moment, who would not be aware of what you were doing. Yes, for you also I wish this "thank you"—and this adieu—to commend you to the God whose face I see in yours.

And may we find each other, happy "good thieves," in Paradise, if it pleases God, the Father of us both. Amen.

# Part III

# WHEN OTHERS DIE

# 1. THE EXPERIENCE OF GRIEF

*For us, the living, our only indisputable experience of death is the death of others, and the images and analyses that seem to speak to us about our own dying are not the same as those that speak to us about the loss of a loved one. Originally published under a pseudonym, his wife named only by the initial "H," A Grief Observed is the close account the English author C. S. Lewis (1898–1963) kept in his diary after the death of his American wife, Joy. In it, he carefully sets down each turn of feeling, each twist of his grief. Painstakingly honest, Lewis examines the way in which we have to struggle not to lose the dead—and the way in which grief rightly serves to keep the dead in our lives.*

# C. S. Lewis, *A Grief Observed*

No one ever told me that grief felt so like fear. I am not afraid, but the sensation is like being afraid. The same fluttering in the stomach, the same restlessness, the yawning. I keep on swallowing.

At other times it feels like being mildly drunk, or concussed. There is a sort of invisible blanket between the world and me. I find it hard to take in what anyone says. Or perhaps, hard to want to take it in. It is so uninteresting. Yet I want the others to be about me. I dread the moments when the house is empty. If only they would talk to one another and not to me.

There are moments, most unexpectedly, when something inside me tries to assure me that I don't really mind so much, not so very much, after all. Love is not the whole of a man's life. I was happy before I ever met H. I've plenty of what are called "resources." People get over these things. Come, I shan't do so badly. One is ashamed to listen to this voice but it seems for a little to be making out a good case. Then comes a sudden jab of red-hot memory and all this common sense vanishes like an ant in the mouth of a furnace.

On the rebound one passes into tears and pathos. Maudlin tears. I almost prefer the moments of agony. These are at least clean and honest. But the bath of self-pity, the wallow, the loathsome sticky-sweet pleasure of indulging it— that disgusts me. And even while I'm doing it I know it leads me to misrepresent H. herself. Give that mood its head and in a few minutes I shall have substituted for the real woman a mere doll to be blubbered over. Thank God the memory of her is still too strong (will it always be too strong?) to let me get away with it.

For H. wasn't like that at all. Her mind was lithe and quick and muscular as a leopard. Passion, tenderness, and pain were all equally unable to disarm it. It scented the first whiff of cant or slush; then sprang, and knocked you over before you knew what was happening. How many bubbles of mine she pricked! I soon learned not to talk rot to her unless I did it for the sheer pleasure—and there's another red-hot jab—of being exposed and laughed at. I was never less silly than as H.'s lover.

And no one ever told me about the laziness of grief. Except at my job— where the machine seems to run on much as usual—I loathe the slightest effort. Not only writing but even reading a letter is too much. Even shaving. What does it matter now whether my cheek is rough or smooth? They say an unhappy man wants distractions—something to take him out of himself. Only as a dog-tired man wants an extra blanket on a cold night; he'd rather lie there shivering than get up and find one. It's easy to see why the lonely become untidy; finally, dirty and disgusting.

Meanwhile, where is God? This is one of the most disquieting symptoms. When you are happy, so happy that you have no sense of needing Him, so happy that you are tempted to feel His claims upon you as an interruption, if you remember yourself and turn to Him with gratitude and praise, you will be—or so it feels—welcomed with open arms. But go to Him when your need is desperate, when all other help is in vain, and what do you find? A door slammed in your face, and a sound of bolting and double bolting on the inside. After that, silence. You may as well turn away. The longer you wait, the more emphatic the silence will become. There are no lights in the windows. It might be an empty house. Was it ever inhabited? It seemed so once. And that seeming was as strong as this. What can this mean? Why is He so present a commander in our time of prosperity and so very absent a help in time of trouble?

I tried to put some of these thoughts to C. this afternoon. He reminded me that the same thing seems to have happened to Christ: "Why hast thou forsaken me?" I know. Does that make it easier to understand?

Not that I am (I think) in much danger of ceasing to believe in God. The real danger is of coming to believe such dreadful things about Him. The conclusion I dread is not "So there's no God after all," but "So this is what God's really like. Deceive yourself no longer."

Our elders submitted and said, "Thy will be done." How often had bitter resentment been stifled through sheer terror and an act of love—yes, in every sense, an act—put on to hide the operation?

Of course it's easy enough to say that God seems absent at our greatest need because He is absent—non-existent. But then why does He seem so present when, to put it quite frankly, we don't ask for Him?

One thing, however, marriage has done for me. I can never again believe that religion is manufactured out of our unconscious, starved desires and is a substitute for sex. For those few years H. and I feasted on love; every mode of it—solemn and merry, romantic and realistic, sometimes as dramatic as a thunderstorm, sometimes as comfortable and unemphatic as putting on your soft slippers. No cranny of heart or body remained unsatisfied. If God were a substitute for love we ought to have lost all interest in Him. Who'd bother about substitutes when he has the thing itself? But that isn't what happens. We both knew we wanted something besides one another—quite a different kind of something, a quite different kind of want. You might as well say that when lovers have one another they will never want to read, or eat, or breathe.

After the death of a friend, years ago, I had for some time a most vivid feeling of certainty about his continued life; even his enhanced life. I have begged to be given even one hundredth part of the same assurance about H. There is no answer. Only the locked door, the iron curtain, the vacuum, absolute zero. Them as asks don't get. I was a fool to ask. For now, even if that assurance came I should distrust it. I should think it a self-hypnosis induced by my own prayers.

At any rate I must keep clear of the spiritualists. I promised H. I would. She knew something of those circles.

Keeping promises to the dead, or to anyone else, is very well. But I begin to see that "respect for the wishes of the dead" is a trap. Yesterday I stopped myself only in time from saying about some trifle "H. wouldn't have liked that." This is unfair to the others. I should soon be using "what H. would have liked" as an instrument of domestic tyranny; with her supposed likings becoming a thinner and thinner disguise for my own.

I cannot talk to the children about her. The moment I try, there appears on their faces neither grief, nor love, nor fear, nor pity, but the most fatal of all nonconductors, embarrassment. They look as if I were committing an indecency. They are longing for me to stop. I felt just the same after my own mother's death when my father mentioned her. I can't blame them. It's the way boys are.

I sometimes think that shame, mere awkward, senseless shame, does as much towards preventing good acts and straightforward happiness as any of our vices can do. And not only in boyhood.

Or are the boys right? What would H. herself think of this terrible little notebook to which I come back and back? Are these jottings morbid? I once read the sentence "I lay awake all night with toothache, thinking about toothache and about lying awake." That's true to life. Part of every misery is, so to speak, the misery's shadow or reflection: the fact that you don't merely suffer but have to keep on thinking about the fact that you suffer. I not only live each endless day in grief, but live each day thinking about living each day in grief. Do these notes merely aggravate that side of it? Merely confirm the monotonous, tread-mill march of the mind round one subject? But what am I to do? I must have some drug, and reading isn't a strong enough drug now. By writing it all down (all?—no: one thought in a hundred) I believe I get a little outside it. That's how I'd defend it to H. But ten to one she'd see a hole in the defense.

It isn't only the boys either. An odd byproduct of my loss is that I'm aware of being an embarrassment to everyone I meet. At work, at the club, in the street, I see people, as they approach me, trying to make up their minds whether they'll "say something about it" or not. I hate it if they do, and if they don't. Some funk it altogether. R. has been avoiding me for a week. I like best the well brought-up young men, almost boys, who walk up to me as if I were a dentist, turn very red, get it over, and then edge away to the bar as quickly as they decently can. Perhaps the bereaved ought to be isolated in special settlements like lepers.

To some I'm worse than an embarrassment. I am a death's head. Whenever I meet a happily married pair I can feel them both thinking, "One or other of us must some day be as he is now."

At first I was very afraid of going to places where H. and I had been happy—our favorite pub, our favorite wood. But I decided to do it at once—like sending a pilot up again as soon as possible after he's had a crash. Unexpectedly, it makes no difference. Her absence is no more emphatic in those places than anywhere else. It's not local at all. I suppose that if one were forbidden all salt one wouldn't notice it much more in any one food than in another. Eating in general would be different, every day, at every meal. It is like that. The act of living is different all through. Her absence is like the sky, spread over everything.

But no, that is not quite accurate, There is one place where her absence comes locally home to me, and it is a place I can't avoid. I mean my own body. It had such a different importance while it was the body of H.'s lover. Now it's like an empty house. But don't let me deceive myself. This body would become important to me again, and pretty quickly, if I thought there was anything wrong with it.

Cancer, and cancer, and cancer. My mother, my father, my wife. I wonder who is next in the queue.

Yet H. herself, dying of it, and well knowing the fact, said that she had lost a great deal of her old horror at it. When the reality came, the name and the idea were in some degree disarmed. And up to a point I very nearly understood. This is important. One never meets just Cancer, or War, or Unhappiness (or Happiness). One only meets each hour or moment that comes. All manner of ups and downs. Many bad spots in our best times, many good ones in our worst. One never gets the total impact of what we call "the thing itself." But we call it wrongly. The thing itself is simply all these ups and downs: the rest is a name or an idea.

It is incredible how much happiness, even how much gaiety, we sometimes had together after all hope was gone. How long, how tranquilly, how nourishingly, we talked together that last night!

And yet, not quite together. There's a limit to the "one flesh." You can't really share someone else's weakness, or fear or pain. What you feel may be bad. It might conceivably be as bad as what the other felt, though I should distrust anyone who claimed that it was. But it would still be quite different. When I speak of fear, I mean the merely animal fear, the recoil of the organism from its destruction; the smothery feeling; the sense of being a rat in a trap. It can't be transferred. The mind can sympathize; the body, less. In one way the bodies of lovers can do it least. All their love passages have trained them to have, not identical, but complementary, correlative, even opposite, feelings about one I another.

We both knew this. I had my miseries, not hers; she had hers, not mine. The end of hers would be the coming-of-age of mine. We were setting out on different roads. This cold truth, this terrible traffic-regulation ("You, Madam, to the right—you, Sir, to the left") is just the beginning of the separation which is death itself.

And this separation, I suppose, waits for all. I have been thinking of H. and myself as peculiarly unfortunate in being torn apart. But presumably all lovers are. She once said to me, "Even if we both died at exactly the same moment, as we lie here side by side, it would be just as much a separation as the one you're so afraid of." Of course she didn't know, any more than I do. But she was near death; near enough to make a good shot. She used to quote "Alone into the Alone." She said it felt like that. And how immensely improbable that it should be otherwise. Time and space and body were the very things that brought us together; the telephone wires by which we communicated. Cut one off, or cut both off simultaneously. Either way, mustn't the conversation stop?

Unless you assume that some other means of communication—utterly different, yet doing the same work—would be immediately substituted. But then, what conceivable point could there be in severing the old ones? Is God a clown who whips away your bowl of soup one moment in order, next moment, to replace it with another bowl of the same soup? Even nature isn't such a clown as that. She never plays exactly the same tune twice.

It is hard to have patience with people who say, "There is no death" or "Death doesn't matter." There is death. And whatever is matters. And whatever happens has consequences, and it and they are irrevocable and irreversible. You might as well say that birth doesn't matter. I look up at the night sky. Is anything more certain than that in all those vast times and spaces, if I were allowed to search them, I should nowhere find her face, her voice, her touch? She died. She is dead. Is the word so difficult to learn?

I have no photograph of her that's any good. I cannot even see her face distinctly in my imagination. Yet the odd face of some stranger seen in a crowd this morning may come before me in vivid perfection the moment I close my eyes tonight. No doubt, the explanation is simple enough. We have seen the faces of those we know best so variously, from so many angles, in so many lights, with so many expressions waking, sleeping, laughing, crying, eating, talking, thinking—that all the impressions crowd into our memory together and cancel out into a mere blur. But her voice is still vivid. The remembered voice—that can turn me at any moment to a whimpering child.

# 2. BURYING THE DEAD

*We do something significant when we perform a funeral—not merely for the living, but for the dead as well. The American civil-rights leader Ralph Abernathy (1926–90) was vice president of the Southern Christian Leadership Conference (SCLC) at the time its president, Dr. Martin Luther King, Jr. (1929–68), was assassinated on April 4, 1968, while planning a march in Memphis, Tennessee. He was also Dr. King's oldest friend and collaborator, and the man who helped the widow, Mrs. Coretta Scott King, plan Dr. King's very public funeral in Atlanta. In the details he relates—the march from Nashville, the search for a pair of mules to haul the bier, the heat, and the crowds—there is a hint of the reason we have funerals at all: to preserve the honor of the dead, to set a final vision of them, and to establish a physical location where they will come always to mind.*

# Ralph Abernathy, *And the Walls Came Tumbling Down*

At about 3 A.M., I suddenly felt the need to get out of the motel—and to be with my friend, who was by now lying all alone in the funeral home. So I found Solomon Jones and pulled him aside.

"Take me to the funeral home," I said.

Ben Hooks overheard and said he would go with me, a gesture I greatly appreciated. Then others said they would go—and so we eventually had several carloads. We wound through the dark streets of Memphis like a dress rehearsal of a funeral procession.

The funeral director met us at the door and offered his hand. He told us it was a very sad occasion and asked how he could help us.

"I'd like to view the body," I said.

He shook his head slowly.

"You don't want to go in right now, Reverend Abernathy," he said.

I assured him that I did.

"I promise you that you don't," he said. "Take my word on it. Please."

But I insisted, so he shook his head sadly and said, "Follow me, but I want to warn you that we have just received the remains from the hospital and haven't had a chance to do our own work."

I nodded, pretending I understood, but I really didn't. Ben Hooks said he would go in with me, and later I was glad he'd do so, though I wonder if he was glad, given the nature of what we saw.

I had never before viewed a corpse that had undergone an autopsy, and I never want to see another. The sight haunts me yet, though for some reason I had to see it, would never have felt I'd satisfied my obligation to Martin if I hadn't seen his body at that moment.

They had cut open his forehead at the hairline and rolled the scalp downward until it covered half his face. Then they had sawed his head open to expose the inside of his skull. What we saw was not a face but the curved dome of a still-glistening brain. I stared for an instant, a mute witness to the final dehumanization of Martin Luther King, Jr., his transformation from person to thing. I knew in that moment that I could leave this body now, leave it forever, because it no longer belonged to my friend. I was ready for the burial.

So I picked a temporary casket and a suit to clothe the body for the trip back to Atlanta. . . .

Calls and telegrams were pouring into the Lorraine Motel and into SCLC headquarters in Atlanta, and one contained an offer from Nelson Rockefeller: He would be happy to make his plane available to us for the return of the body to Atlanta. It was not only a gracious gesture, but it solved a practical problem for us and made it possible for the family and close friends to accompany the body.

When it was time to go to the airport, we drove in a procession to the funeral home, where we found hundreds of reporters and photographers taking pictures of the open casket. As soon as we arrived, the funeral director closed the casket and some of the staff carried it to the waiting hearse as the rest of us climbed into waiting limousines and drove in a slow processional to the airport.

Governor Rockefeller's plane had not yet arrived, and as we walked forward, ahead of the casket, I saw Coretta, standing, waiting. When she saw me she moved forward.

As I recall, there were about thirty-five of us on the plane, with the casket in the rear. It was a solemn trip, and most of us stared out the window and thought our own thoughts. As for me, I thought about Juanita and the children—and how they might have felt had it been my body en route to Atlanta in a metal box. I also thought about the future, already crowding in on me with measuring tape, ready to fit me for the next casket.

But as the plane banked and then nosed downward toward Atlanta, I thought again of Martin and what he had said as we took off only three days earlier—the brittle smile on his face when the captain announced the bomb threat and reassured us that everything was safe. There had been normal and very human fear behind that smile. Now, he was unworried, at peace. For just an instant, staring at the greening woods below and thinking of what was to come, I almost envied him. . . .

The days immediately following Martin's death were filled with anguish and hard work. We all knew that despite our private grief we would be the central figures in a tremendously important public occasion, the nearest thing in our history to a state funeral for a black. Coretta set a strong example for the rest of us. She was controlled and efficient during the planning and execution of the details, with help from everybody, including Daddy King, who was surprisingly calm in the midst of a tragedy he had been dreading for so many years.

Together we decided that the body, after being prepared at Bell Street Funeral Home, would lie in state at Sisters Chapel at Spelman College. Then on Tuesday there would be two separate ceremonies, one service in the church, the other a public memorial service to be held outdoors at Morehouse College, almost five miles away from Ebenezer Baptist Church. All plans were conditioned by the fact that literally tens of thousands of people would be coming from all over the country and that most of the black people in Atlanta would probably want to take part in some way. Clearly the Morehouse ceremony would accommodate the many simple people, white as well as black, who wanted to pay tribute to Martin, while the church funeral would be for family, friends, and a few dignitaries of national prominence. Coretta asked me to officiate at both services, and of course I agreed. She also asked me to conduct the committal service at the grave side.

Meanwhile, I had a congregation to face on Sunday and a march to lead on Monday back in Memphis. In many ways the West Hunter service on Sunday would be more difficult than officiating at the three events on Tuesday. "Officiating" meant acting as a kind of master of ceremonies, but at West Hunter I would have to stand before my congregation and talk about Martin's death—its meaning to me, its implications for the nation, and its religious significance. I wasn't sure I could sort out all these meanings so soon after the event, but on Friday evening and Saturday I had to try.

On Sunday morning, I mounted the pulpit and delivered my sermon in the form of a letter to Martin, which I shared with my congregation. I called it "A Short Letter to My Dearest Friend in the City Called Heaven."

As plans for the funeral began to crystallize, we found that their implementation was sometimes more difficult than the planners had anticipated. For example, to emphasize Martin's commitment to the poor people of the nation, we decided to have the casket transported from Ebenezer Church to Morehouse on a cart drawn by two mules. Many people still remember the stark and grim image of the cortege rolling down the streets of Atlanta; as a symbol, the mules and cart had served their purpose. But they had not been easy to come by.

We had to search the countryside before we found two mules who could work in tandem. I put Hosea Williams in charge, and he must have driven up a hundred red clay roads searching for a pair. Finally he found what he was looking for and was able to persuade the owner to lend them to us for a day. But the cart turned out to be even more elusive.

Finally, on Sunday afternoon, Hosea came by the church to give me the news.

"Well," he said with a sigh of relief, "we've got a wagon."

"Where did you get it?" I asked.

"At a farm about thirty miles down the road. Remote place."

"Did you have any trouble talking the owner into letting you have it?"

"No," he said evenly. "I stole it."

I couldn't believe my ears.

"You stole the cart!"

He nodded grimly.

"Nothing else to do. Nobody was around, and I couldn't take the chance they'd say no."

I tried not to think about it. I could imagine the owner as he watched the funeral on television suddenly recognizing the wagon and leaping to his feet in rage. Before the casket reached Morehouse he might be there with an officer and a warrant.

"We'll have to find the owner as quickly as possible and pay him for the wagon," I said.

"Yes," said Hosea gravely. "We'll have to do that."

The funeral was on Tuesday, but first we went back to Memphis to make our nonviolent march along the same route we had hoped to follow when the Invaders had begun their disruptive tactics. Instead of singing hymns, we would be marching silently in tribute to Martin. While we hoped that what had happened already would discourage any further violence, we had no idea what the atmosphere in Memphis might be. There were people who might well find that the spilling of one man's blood had only whetted their appetite for more violence and death.

My fears were unfounded. It was a memorable occasion, proving that black people could conduct a nonviolent march in Memphis, Tennessee. . . . I remember walking down Main Street, seeing the somber and grieving faces of the black people lined on either curb, and then the white faces, some pained and others enigmatic, all of them clearly anxious in the wake of the terrible event of the previous week. For the first time, I had to wonder if the next person I passed wouldn't pull out a gun and start blasting away or if a bullet fired from some distant window wouldn't suddenly tear into my head, even before I heard the sound of the shot. . . .

On Tuesday we buried Martin. . . . I remember looking out at the crowd sitting solemnly at attention, and thinking that something was wrong with the scene, though for a moment I couldn't figure out what it was. Then I realized: This was Ebenezer Church, yet most of the people jamming the pews were white. So many politicians and celebrities had come for the funeral that there wasn't room for all of Martin's friends and relatives, the people who came to this very church to hear him preach on Sundays. Fortunately, they would have their opportunity to see and hear a memorial service at Morehouse later in the afternoon.

But I began the service by pointing out that we were here to bury a man rather than make a political statement, though I acknowledged the larger importance of Martin's death. I didn't want to offend those present, but I wanted to point out the essentially religious nature of what was about to happen and to remind them that a funeral is a very private and very personal occasion.

Perhaps the most moving moment came near the beginning of the service when they played a tape recording of Martin's instructions concerning his own funeral. Excerpted from a sermon he had delivered at this same church, the words were almost too painful to bear.

"If any of you are around when I have to meet my day, I don't want a long funeral. And if you get somebody to deliver the eulogy, tell him not to talk too long. . . .

"I'd like somebody to mention that day that Martin Luther King, Jr., tried to give his life serving others.

"I'd like for somebody to say that day that Martin Luther King, Jr., tried to love somebody. . . .

"I want you to be able to say that day that I did try to feed the hungry. I want you to be able to say that day that I did try in my life to clothe the naked. I want you to say on that day that I did try in my life to visit those who were in prison. And I want you to say that I tried to love and serve humanity." . . .

At the end of the service I led the congregation outside reading the words of the Twenty-third Psalm, and we watched as the pallbearers—members of the SCLC executive staff who had helped him build the organization—lifted the highly polished mahogany casket onto the wagon and saw the mules lean forward and begin to pull their load down the street. Fifty thousand people followed behind while another one hundred thousand watched along the way.

The walk from Ebenezer to Morehouse was almost five miles and the heat was merciless. With the funeral lasting an hour longer than scheduled and with the strenuous march and blazing sun, it was small wonder that by the time we got to the Morehouse campus, people were beginning to pass out.

I had hoped to be able to start as soon as we arrived, but the crowd was milling around and talking as if they were at a lawn party rather than at a formal ceremony. When the family arrived, however, they surged around them; and we had chaotic shouting and screaming for about ten minutes.

At that point I wasn't certain we would be able to hold the memorial service. I thought of the mob at Memphis on the first day when Martin had suddenly shouted "Call off the march!" I had that same sense of panic.

Obviously, others felt the same way, because people in the crowd began to faint and medics were kept busy carrying them off in stretchers. As I began to speak, I heard the cry of someone else keeling over, and when I tried to carry on, Daddy King jumped to his feet and called out, "Ralph, you've got to get this over! People are dying!" . . .

Mercifully, the four-mile journey to South View Cemetery was made by motorcade, with the hearse and family limousines leading the way. Most of the political celebrities had quietly slipped off, either after the church service or after the memorial service, but crowds of simple and anonymous black people were lined on both sides of the road to salute Martin one last time.

The old cemetery, its sternly erect tombstones scattered over a green hill-side, was also crowded with people, most of them black, a good many of them close friends and associates. We were like Gideon's army now. All the faint-hearted had fallen by the wayside.

By this time I was exhausted, as was everyone else, so I made it brief and from the heart, the way those of us in the black Baptist church do it best. Consequently, I don't have a text of my remarks. But one newspaper account contained the following excerpt. "This cemetery is too small for his spirit but we submit his body to the ground. The grave is too narrow for his soul, but we commit his body to the ground. No coffin, no crypt, no stone can hold his greatness. But we submit his body to the ground." At that moment I bade him a silent goodbye and turned my back on the grave, determined to make his spirit live in the army and marching orders he had left behind.

But it turned out that I had not really committed his body to the ground, at least not permanently. For I was to see him one more time—not figuratively, but literally.

After the funeral and readjustment to life without him, Coretta decided to build a center in memory of Martin, an institution to carry on his work. I had encouraged her to become active in the SCLC and had even prepared an office for her in our headquarters. But she wanted to pursue the future independently, and certainly there were many donors who were eager to contribute to a fitting memorial for Martin.

So with seventy-five thousand dollars from the Ebenezer Baptist Church and seventy-five thousand dollars that the SCLC contributed, she bought a piece of property next door to the Ebenezer Church, and went forward with plans to build the Martin Luther King, Jr., Center for Nonviolent Social Change. One of the things she intended to do during construction was to relocate Martin's body in a tomb on the grounds of the center, on an island in the middle of a small manmade lake.

So I was not really surprised when she called me one day and asked me to accompany her and other members of the immediate family to exhume the body and move it.

"I'll be happy to be there," I said. "When will it be?"

"Tonight," she said. "We'll meet at 2:00 A.M. at South View Cemetery, so there won't be any curiosity seekers."

It was a dark night when we gathered on that hillside and stood there, watching as the cemetery and funeral home workers, illuminated by flashlights, unsealed the mausoleum and slid the casket out. Coretta, A. D., Christine,

Daddy King, Isaac Farris and a few other close family members were there, and we stood in silence as the men swiftly and efficiently carried the still glossy casket and installed it in the hearse. Then we followed behind—a three-car entourage winding along the dark road into the sleeping city.

When we got to the funeral home, the family went into a waiting room, but A. D. and I accompanied the casket into the back. The man in charge then explained to me what they had to do.

"When we removed the casket from the chapel at Spelman, we didn't have time to seal it properly. So that's what we're going to do now. We'll take off the top, put glue on it, and then press the top back on. It will take about ten minutes."

I started to leave, then something made me stay—a vague sense of responsibility to Martin. As his best friend, I couldn't allow his body to suffer this last indignity at the hands of strangers. So I stood and watched with A. D. as they took the hinges off the lid and lifted it from the casket.

Then I saw him, lying there underneath a thin sheet of glass. His face, his features were still intact—solemn, though perhaps a little pinched, as if he had suffered a long, long illness. But his shoes and pant legs were covered with green moss. As I looked, my eyes riveted on the figure lying there, I realized that the sight of his corpse disturbed me less now than the first time I saw it lying under the brown paper in the Memphis morgue, a tag tied on its toe.

They worked quickly, efficiently to clean off the moss, paint the lid with glue, then fit it back on the casket, several of them pressing down with their full weight to make sure the bonding was perfect. Then, when they had finished, the man in charge nodded to me and A. D.

"That should do it," he said. "He should last two hundred years now."

As we left the room I thought that if history was just, he would last a good deal longer than that in the minds and hearts of his people.

# 3. DYING ALONE

*A plague, in a culture's experience, is always more horrible in the fact that many are dying from the same cause. And the deaths from the contemporary plague of AIDS—the disease that attacks the immune system and thus allows innumerable other cancers and diseases to attack the body—are so horrible that the disease itself seems to many to be a thing more significant than the individuals it kills. In her 1996 account of a friend's death from AIDS, however, the writer and editor Alane Saliemo Mason refuses to lose the particularity of the sufferer in the generality of his disease. Struggling to keep hold of her friend in her grief, she keeps coming back to the fact that every one of us dies alone—and every death is the unique loss of a real, singular person.*

# Alane Salierno Mason, "Reconciliation of Unbelief"

Last night I again met him in my dreams. He was sitting on the steps of a church, wearing a thin shirt and shivering a bit in the cold. I chastised him for not wearing a jacket; I was still so conscious of the danger of his getting sick. Then we went inside the church, and held each other tightly in the back corner for a long time. I could feel his whole body, living and warm, against mine, the pressure of my arm around him and his around me, the tops of our thighs meeting. It was an embrace that was a completed and completely physical expression of love, an embodiment of it, physical but not sexual, and in it was resolved the entire thirteen-year history of our friendship.

Then he was in Jerusalem with me, the earthly, not the heavenly city, and for a moment I was preoccupied, as I have been in dreams before, by the difference between authentic and inauthentic relics.

When we were both in college, in North Carolina, the campus was flooded with evangelists who would interrupt your solitary reveries on a step or a wall or a path to ask, "Have you been saved?" A fellow freshman told me that, as a Catholic, I would go to hell for worshiping the Virgin Mary. Another student asked me, "Don't you want to be sure that if you were to walk out onto that highway and be hit by a car right now, you would be going to heaven? That's what it means to be saved." I said no, not really, I did not want to be sure. I said I believed that doubt was part of faith and uncertainty part of hope; that I felt in me a faith I wanted to share, just by living, with my friends, most of whom for all I knew were agnostics or atheists. She said, maybe you need to get different friends.

He was elusive then. He reminded me of a deer running in the woods. He lived more dangerously than I. Away from our dorm we saw each other only intermittently, passing an afternoon sitting on a wall in the sun discussing books and classes, or listening to a lunchtime Bach concert in the Episcopal church. We cooked in the tiny dorm kitchen no one ever seemed to use; pan-tossed angel hair pasta with vegetables, egg pastina with butter (from my childhood), cheese grits and pork chops (from his), extravagant omelets (he showed me how they puffed up more if you cooked them with a lid on the pan). He taught me how to make sourdough biscuits; we rolled them on my desk and cut them with a glass. From the beginning I considered him one of my best friends. When he heard this during our freshman year he was surprised; he said I had not yet risked anything with him. It was the first time anyone had suggested to me that friendship had to do with risk and not security. Later, I would try to tell him everything I thought, to risk all in words, and often failed, especially at the end.

He retained a privacy that was no longer an elusiveness, no longer hiding from himself and others, just a staking out of a territory that was his own.

For a while after he moved to a new city and began to explore not just gay sex but a gay life, and since we both worked at jobs that did not pay us enough to travel, we did not see each other very often. When we began to spend time together again, we talked about our uncertainties and frustrations over boyfriends and work; but we also talked about belief and doubt, about the cynicism of intellectuals. The dryness of the world we had seen and of which we could so easily become a part. He scorned superficial pieties, but he was afraid of becoming cynical. He did not want to give up the capacity to believe, the richness and beauty of the Catholic church in which he too had been raised, his spiritual life, his responsibility to what he would choose to call his soul.

We began to go to church together when I was in town. He would not take Communion, so as not to be a hypocrite, as I suppose I was. He respected the rules of the church that allowed him few options, that would have preferred he marry only part of himself to a woman like me, rather than live all in the life to which his heart and body led him. Once at Mass with another friend standing between us, I glanced over, tears in my eyes from some romantic grief, to see that he was crying too.

The mysterious gut infection that brought a pain that made suicide understandable, a pain that filled his entire consciousness, leaving no room for anything but pain.

In talking of this he told me of trying to imagine his death, and in the telling I felt he had made it beautiful. "What do you mean?" he asked quietly. I tried to say that the essential beauty of his way of describing things, and the importance to me of his telling, transfigured them. I could not say, though I felt it, that our conversation itself was a sacrament.

The additional burden of leaving a written legacy was one he both did, and did not, need. He had just left his job to work full-time on his master's thesis when he died, the final infection with its attendant septicemia taking him in a day.

When I asked him a couple of months before if he had ever thought of publishing his journals he almost spat, no. Who would be interested? he said, which I took to mean he would let us decide, after his death, whether anyone was. He loathed sloppiness, self-indulgence when it came to serious work, so he avoided taking his most important work seriously. At his famous friend's insistence he wrote a piece for his magazine, a special issue on AIDS, but the piece never ran. To be honest, it was not right. What was outrageous and brilliant and defiant in a letter to the friend became tame and opaque and self-conscious in the imagined context of a prestigious mainstream magazine. He was not satisfied with it. The problem, he said, was how to find a voice, a form, that could exist in a public space. His art was relentlessly private, journals and letters written with incandescent intensity to an audience of one, or no one; homemade cards, sketches, collages, scatter-paintings, woodblock prints, found-art reliefs and oils, piano sonatas and jazz improvisations, home-cooked meals, snacks of pickled okra and sandwiches of pimento cheese. He invented hilarious anecdotes about his trips to the store, recounted overheard snatches of conversation with relish. After his death, his partner talked about how much time they had spent together "doing nothing special," how good that was. When I visited he made the best coffee, with cream; sometimes he brought it to me in bed, and sat on the foot of the bed, talking me awake for an hour or two. Sometimes we walked around the neighborhood, sat by the fountain, went into a bookstore; once we each got a pair of shoes repaired.

He loved yard sales and flea markets, the castaways of other lives furnishing his own: the sheets, the dishes and cookware, the coffee maker, books, religious artifacts (a plaster Joseph, or is it Anthony? with a rusted chain halo, and Mary, gracing either end of the living room window, which looked over the city in an apartment where several times a day you'd hear a chorus of church bells ringing), the couch and chairs and little marble-topped end table. He had his own yard sales, returning the no-longer-wanted materials of his own life to the reincarnating cycles of secondhand commerce. The profits would go to buy himself and his friends a good dinner.

Perhaps among his papers there is a masterpiece not yet seen or recognized; perhaps we will be able to put a book together from his journals and letters, to which this may serve as introduction; perhaps his famous friend, in a book on friendship, will immortalize him.

Contain him. This jumping out at us from books he read and music he loved and food he relished, things he made us buy, coming to us in our dreams to wrestle us out of sleep into a lake of cold water (as he tried to do to me, mischievously, when he had only been a couple of months dead) or in others' memories of him, alive and rolling naked in a pile of leaves in the park, orchestrating a seduction to "The Girl from Ipanema," getting young women to pose topless for his sketchbook when he was still only twelve ("I could always tell he was different," his mother said, "he could draw a perfect basket of Easter eggs when he was three years old"), what kind of immortality is that?

In the myth-making stories we told in the days after he left us, carving the grooves in our memories that might hold him, the images began to conflict, or if not to contradict, at least to separate from each other, like the planes in the Picasso print that once hung in his kitchen. . . . I do not think he believed in the immortality of art, though he devoured it, honored it, yearned for it. But maybe he did believe in it, and regretted the lack of time to make "a lasting contribution." Maybe he simultaneously believed and did not believe. It is possible he believed that art was no more immortal than the shape of him in the clothes his mother so wanted to bring home with her after he died. Than the taste of her melt-in-the-mouth Yorkshire puddings. The sperm, even, that carried the virus. Perhaps his body itself lives longer than art, in the molecules of him now diffused through the Gulf of Mexico.

In any case there was little division in him between matter and spirit.

His last two years, after he knew he was sick, his innermost circle of friends were all Catholic. Observant and nonobservant, atheist, agnostic and devout, gay, lesbian, and hetero, fornicators all. His hometown priest, singing Broadway show tunes after the scattering of the ashes, saw his mother each week in steadfast prayer to Mary, and thought of her strength as that of the Virgin Mother herself. After he died I would think of the quality of his attentiveness as an aspect of the personality of Christ. Of unlimited conversations with him in eternity as the only conception I could have of heaven. At his deathbed we all prayed, and all partook of the Communion of his last rites. The love of him filled the room. His big toe was turning white as his heart slowly stopped beating—I saw when his brother lifted a corner of the sheet. "Push on out from shore," one of his brothers said, "you're going to a better place"; "you're going to be with God," his most devout gay friend said. Where is that? I thought, what does it mean, to go to be with God? His gay doctor, who had turned the monitor away so that only he had to see it, told us finally that his heart had stopped.

Either he was rolling naked in the leaves somewhere else, and would do so eternally (but without repetition), or he would never do so again. It is difficult to know, isn't it, what we are meant to understand by "the resurrection of the body"?

When we all jumped in the water after pouring his ashes off the boat (not scattering, pouring, clouding the water like milk. "Heavy, isn't it?" his father had said of the black nylon bag, full of his "remains"), the thickness of the water on my tongue shocked me, and for a moment I thought I was tasting his ashes. The heavy taste of the salt water like blood. His father's pale face where he drifted alone among the white carnations we had thrown, already swept by the current away from the boat, toward the Gulf.

He had trouble imagining it, he had said, his death. When he tried to contemplate an end to his own existence he was simply mystified by it. He could not understand it. He imagined the grief of his family and friends and was saddened, but when he thought of himself, of his own death, it was not unpleasant. Nor pleasant. When he was a child and couldn't sleep, he used to imagine his mother's womb before sperm and egg had met to form him, then his parents before they met and were married, and each of his parents in their mothers' wombs, and their parents before they were married, in their mothers' wombs, and his grandparents' parents before they met, unraveling the thread of his own existence until he fell asleep. His imagination of his death, he said, was something like that. His death.

He was physically beautiful, and remained so even in death, pale hair dusting strong freckled forearms.

He believed in God, and did not believe, and awaited the reconciliation of his unbelief.

He was afraid of dying.

There was little division in him between matter and spirit.

# 4. WATCHING OTHERS DIE

*"Death does indeed reveal itself as a loss, but the loss is experienced only by those who remain," writes Martin Heidegger, the twentieth-century philosopher and founder of existentialism. We are indeed linked to one another by death—but since each of must die alone, the way in which death links us is in the experience of grief and watching others die. We must recognize, Peter De Vries (1910–93) writes, "The recognition of how long, how long is the mourners' bench upon which we sit, arms linked in undeluded friendship—all of us, brief links, ourselves, in the eternal pity." An American writer best known for his comic and pun-filled novels, De Vries wrote* The Blood of the Lamb *after the death of his young daughter from leukemia. Fictionalizing himself under the name "Wanderhope," he recounts in brilliant detail the appearance of the disease, the suffering of the child, and his grief after her death. In a remarkable passage, he tells of wandering out after her unexpectedly quick death . . . but no, you must read it for yourself.*

# Peter De Vries, *The Blood of the Lamb*

I had to carry Carol to the car for this trip to the hospital. The conviction that one was being systematically tortured revived with the report from Dr. Cameron that the pathologist making the aspiration had used a syringe not precisely dry, vitiating the specimen. We went back the next day, with Carol in such discomfort that Mrs. Brodhag came along to hold the girl's head in her lap and soothe her brow, while she told her stories and jokes. That evening we were rewarded with a telephone call from Dr. Cameron saying that he had been in touch with the pathologist and would be over directly with the report.

Mrs. Brodhag monkeyed about in her kitchen, from a window of which she could see the doctor drive up. She told me later she knew what he had to say from the way he sat in his car a moment before getting out, giving his coat collar a kind of adjustment. He entered the house swinging his bag, somewhat like a hammer thrower in a weight contest preparing to see how far he could hurl it, and he smiled as he marched upstairs first to see the patient. I waited in the living room with my hand locked around a glass of whiskey. When he returned, shouting bluff instructions about dropping those coloring books and keeping up with our homework, he noticed Mrs. Brodhag still hanging about. He dispatched her on some sickroom errand or other that left the two of us together. He hesitated a moment, giving some such flirt to his coat lapels as Mrs. Brodhag must have noted, but at last spoke the word whose utterance could no longer be postponed. We both remained standing for the verdict.

"Baxter and I have been going over these slides at the hospital," he said, his voice slowing as he neared the name on which I knew now I was to be skewered, "and there seems to be a strong suggestion of leukemia."

*The future is a thing of the past.* I still fancy that that was what went through my mind then, precisely in those words, though they were a remark of Stein's, whom I was not to meet till a week later "on the barricades," as he called the parental get-togethers in the Children's Pavilion at Westminster Hospital.

"Fix me one of those, would you? . . . Thanks. Now here's the thing. We have the world's leading authorities on its childhood forms right here in New York. You will take her in to Dr. Scoville tomorrow—"

"Can they do anything for it?"

"My dear boy, where have you been the last ten years? There are first of all the steroids—cortisone and ACTH—which give a quick remission. The minute she's pulled back to normal with those, Dr. Scoville will switch her to the first of the long-range drugs, some of which he's helped develop himself If they should wear off, there's but let's cross those bridges when we come to them." Dr. Cameron cleared his throat in the emphatic manner of one too busy to concern himself with matters that far in the future. "Now the first thing is to see that Carol does her homework so she'll pass into sixth grade without any hitch. Business as usual, that's the ticket. There isn't so much of the school year left that you can't help her through, but if you want, the town will furnish a tutor. Mrs. Quentin is excellent and won't talk. She won't even ask any questions."

"How long do these remissions last?"

The doctor described a circle so large the ice cubes rattled in his glass. "Years . . . "

"And by that time—"

"Of course! They're working on it day and night, and they're bound to get it soon." He jerked his head toward where he knew the telephone to be, and with an almost barroom-buddy solemnity said, "Chances are when I call Scoville to make an appointment for you he won't be home but at the laboratory with his rats. Oh, they'll get it! It's only a question of time, and that we've got on our side. As I say, ten years ago, nothing. Now a great deal. Look. Get this picture firmly fixed in your mind to the exclusion of everything else: Carol going off to school again next September. I promise it. On my solemn oath."

We stood side by side at the window, where he paused a moment to distill if possible a greater degree of optimism between us, hitting thereby upon a tender little irony which he hoped would please me as much as it did him.

"When she graduates from junior high, you'll still be a worried father." He took a copious pull on his drink and gestured toward the playground at the bottom of the yard on which the view here gave. "You might make sure those swings and things are in good working order. And the porch of that playhouse looks a little rickety to me. Have a carpenter check it if you're not a do-it-yourself man. After all, we don't want anything to happen to our girl," he said, and, turning, gave me a shy, almost boyish smile, as though he were offering me the key to courage. . . .

We passed in due course the church of St. Catherine, from which a pair of people were contentedly emerging after their evening devotionals. Here a vibration of anger escaped Stein that was not put into words, but that I felt had given me a flash of illumination into his spirit . . . Stein resented the sedative power of religion, or rather the repose available to those blissfully ignorant that the medicament was a fictitious blank. In this exile from peace of mind to which his reason doomed him, he was like an insomniac driven to awaken sleepers from dreams illegitimately won by going around shouting, "Don't you realize it was a placebo!" Thus it seemed to me that what you were up against in Stein was not logic rampant, but frustrated faith. He could not forgive God for not existing.

When we returned to the Pavilion of Children, Mrs. Stein greeted us in the corridor. "You should see the two of them playing together," she said. "Come look."

We stood in the recreation room doorway. In a pandemonium of television noise, piano music being thumped out by a volunteer as youngsters banged drums and shook tambourines to its rhythm, Rachel and Carol sat side by side at a table, twisting into being paper flowers for children less fortunate. Mrs. Stein had quoted that bit as we came down the hall with a surprising minimum of rue. "Aren't they just too sweet together?" she beamed in the doorway.

"Lifelong friends," said Stein, who gave, and asked, no quarter.

My conversations with Stein are almost all I am recalling of my relations with other parents because they were vital to my concerns, not because they and the brief skirmish I overheard in the lounge were typical of human inter-course there. Far from it. Airing the absolutes is no longer permitted in polite society, save where a Stein and a Wanderhope meet and knock their heads to-gether, but I do not think this is due to apathy or frivolity, or because such pursuits are vain, though one pant for God as the hart after water-brooks. There is another reason why we chatter of this and that while our heads burn within us.

We live this life by a kind of conspiracy of grace: the common assumption, or pretense, that human existence is "good" or "matters" or has "meaning," a glaze of charm or humor by which we conceal from one another and perhaps even ourselves the suspicion that it does not, and our conviction in times of trouble that it is overpriced, something to be endured rather than enjoyed. No-where does this function more than in precisely such a slice of hell as a Chil-dren's Pavilion, where the basic truths would seem to mock any state of mind other than rage and despair. Rage and despair are indeed carried about in the heart, but privately, to be let out on special occasions, like savage dogs for ex-ercise, occasions in solitude when God is cursed, birds stoned from the trees or the pillow hammered in darkness. In the ward lounge itself, a scene in which a changing collection of characters are waiting for a new medicine that might as well be called Godot, the conversation is indistinguishable from that going on at the moment in the street, a coffee break at the office from which one is absent, or a dinner party to which one could not accept an invitation. Even the exchange of news about their children has often the quality of gossip. An ear-ful of it would be incredible to an uninvolved spectator, not to its principals. Quiet is requested for the benefit of the other parents. One holds his peace in obedience to a tacit law as binding as if it were framed on a corridor wall with a police officer on hand to see that it was enforced: "No fuss." This is all perhaps nothing more than the principle of sportsmanship at its highest, given in return for the next man's. Even Stein had it in no small degree, for all his seeming refusal to wish me good hunting in my spiritual quest. Perhaps he was trying to tell me in as nice a way as he could that there was no game in those woods. His grim little jokes on the barricades were in their way part of this call to courage.

But while human abilities to sustain this sportsmanship vary, none is unlimited. Twice I had the uneasy experience of witnessing a crackup in the ranks of those one comes to think of, not too farfetchedly, as one's outfit—that moment when the thin membrane to which our sanity is entrusted splits and breaks asunder, spilling violence in every direction.

There was a mother Carol and I saw in every hospitalization, taking care of a four-year-old boy who was by now a scarecrow. She lived in Ohio, and her husband came only on weekends, or when he could get off from work. Her name was May Schwartz, and her comely Jewish bulk, her ripe yolky warmth and vitality typified a certain order of female appeal, often irresistible to the Gentile eye. Though she was neither very young nor notably shapely any more, one always marked her passage down the corridor. Wearing high heels to offset her short height, rather than the "sensible" shoes that would certainly have eased her thousand marches to and from her vegetable, she would bounce along with a towel and wash basin or a glass of soda pop in her hands, and return any nod of greeting, as you passed her wheeling your own charge, by smiling and rolling her eyes up to the ceiling as if to say, "Gawd." I heard her say it aloud when told in the lounge that a rabbi had arrived to call on Sammy, rolling her eyes again as she rose to receive him. I happened to see the rabbi go into Sammy's room, where he put on a black skullcap and stood at the foot of the bed murmuring something, before thrusting the cap back into his overcoat pocket and hurrying away again, looking a little foolish. Mrs. Schwartz said that her husband arranged for these pastoral visits, in which she "saw no harm."

One night I was sleeping on the leather couch in the lounge, or trying to. I was too excited by the news, just acquired, that I might take Carol home tomorrow. I was staying overnight so that we could make an early start in the morning. . . . There was a stir behind the thin wall separating the lounge from the next room, where Mrs. Schwartz spent her nights on a cot. Then I heard the door of that room open. The faint scuff of slippered feet followed, and Mrs. Schwartz herself stood in the open doorway of the lounge. She had on a flannel robe, under which could be seen the legs of a pair of pajamas. Her face was invisible since the lounge was dark, but against the faint glow cast by a corridor light I could see her arms go up and knew that she had her own hands to her face. From her motionless figure now issued a series of broken, muffled sounds very similar I now sensed, as a chill went up my spine, to those that had a moment ago greeted her own ears. . . . She was, in any case, not the solid rock for which we had been accustomed to take her.

As she came forward into the room I rose. She whispered for me not to do so, urging me back down onto the couch with a force that dropped me abruptly once more on the leather cushion. She sank to her knees and began suddenly to beat the arm of the couch with both fists, at the same time babbling incoherently. The words came out in a stream, English, Yiddish, oaths and imprecations, blasphemies and entreaties I could not hope to reproduce. "All they can do is kill mice!" she said in a kind of whispered scream. I grasped her shoulders, and, when this did no good, her wrists. Whereupon she wrenched her arms free and threw them around my neck, in a spasm of emotion that might have been mistaken, by someone glancing into the darkened room, for an amorous clutch. Which in a mad sort of way it probably was. For as suddenly as she had begun she stopped, went to a chair, blew her nose, and said, "It's a funny thing about two people going through something like this. There are things husband and wife just can't tell each other that they can a third person."

"Tell" each other! I thought, what in God's name has she told me? As if sensing this, she immediately added, "I guess I mean do to each other. You have no wife, but I've got news for you. You think you could have shared this?" She shook her head, and though the illumination from the corridor was too dim for me to make out her face, I could imagine her shrugged mouth and closed eyes. "Two people can't share unhappiness. You think probably if you had her, 'Well, we could go through this together. It would bring us closer together. Leaning on each other.'" Again the headshake, with news for me. "They lean away from each other. Two people can't share grief. In fact—" She broke off, as though momentarily debating the prudence of the revelation on the tip of her tongue, then making it anyway. "In some ways it drives them apart, an explosion between them. No, that's not it either." She lowered her head, and for a moment I feared a revival of hysterics. She went on, as though the paradox of what she was elucidating was an aid to objectivity, "When this first came to us, was fresh, the wound, there were times when I resented my husband. Because he, what's the word I want?" She snapped her fingers. "Presumed. Presumed to share what was basically a woman's grief. Horning in on a sorrow the woman is sole proprietor of. Isn't that ridiculous? But there it is, a chapter in what's this man's name who writes about the war between the sexes. Can you beat it?" she softly cried, bringing her fist down ominously now on the arm of the chair, but only once, and that like a public speaker, or actor, well in control of his effects. I sat mesmerized in my own seat, transfixed in perhaps the most amazing midnight I had ever lived through; yet one possessing, in the dreamy dislocations of which it formed a part, a weird, bland naturalness like that of a Chirico landscape, full of shadows infinitely longer than the objects casting them. "And no doubt Schwartz has some of the same resentment as mine. Never is this stated between two people, but it's there. Driving this wedge between them, so that a woman can't break down to her husband but she can very well fling herself for a moment on another man's breast, while Schwartz at this very minute is probably with that . . . Well, never mind. Does this make sense to you?"

"Why, I think I can see where . . . "

"Well then make room in your head for the exact opposite explanation. That we keep outbursts from one another because we owe it to the other person. Out of a feeling for the other party. We owe it to them not to wish on them what they keep from us in their own moments. All this you're learning about marriage," she went on, like a chiropractor manipulating his subject's head in a series of violent, though supposedly salubrious, contrasts. "So your wife," she went on in a manner suggesting that she absorbed as much gossip as she dispensed in these watches of the night, "would never have come to you in the way I just did. To somebody else maybe, yes, but to you, no." She brushed at her cheeks and rose. "So now how about a cigarette?" She turned to switch on the light, glancing then at the electric coffee urn always standing on a table there, to see if it was connected. "Let's plug this thing in and heat up what's in it."

As we smoked a cigarette and drank our coffee, she told me something about her husband's work. He was publicity director for an Akron shoe factory, much prized by the firm though beset by envious rivals waiting to ambush him. She hoped we would get a chance to meet when next he came to the hospital. We would probably have a lot to say to each other.

The second drama was of a different sort and by no means as instructive, except on a more elementary level.

Off the main corridor was a room in which the doctors held daily consultations among themselves on all the cases then on the floor, and into which individual ones sometimes drew parents for a word in private. One day as I walked past its closed door, I heard behind it a shrill man's voice upbraiding somebody. "Then why didn't you switch to the other drug sooner, you—" The epithet, if such it was, was drowned out by the scraping of a chair. This became immediately an unmistakable scuffle, in which shouts and overturned chairs mingled in equal measure. I froze, wondering whether to rush in. I had heard that crazed parents on rare occasions physically attacked their children's doctors, and indeed had once noticed an armed guard unobtrusively but watchfully haunting the ward. I could understand this behavior as an exaggeration of a normal reaction, perhaps even a normal irrationality, from a disquieting sensation that had suddenly gone through me the evening Dr. Cameron had come to the house with his news. *I had hated him physically.* I had wanted to bash his teeth in. The vituperation continued, varied only by counterprotestations and pleas to "control yourself" in a voice now recognizable as that of Dr. Scoville. When an especially alarming thud was heard, I opened the door and ran in.

Dr. Scoville, in his white coat, was standing behind a desk, which he had evidently been circling to keep between himself and his client—a man I recognized as an out-of-town father whom I had seen wheeling a child in a perambulator. He had red hair and bulging blue eyes that gave him a look of subdued frenzy the best of times. Now his face resembled a pot of tomatoes about to boil over. There was an X ray on an illuminated panel, whose portents the doctor had probably been trying to interpret when the man had gone out of control. In a blaze of deprecation now broadened to include the hospital, to which he should never have removed his child from the one in New Jersey, he shouted, "—progress! I understand you can now induce malignancies in normal tissues!" I stepped in at this point and tried to calm him. This made him turn on me, perhaps in a kind of escape; he may have sensed by now that he was making a spectacle of himself, as we sometimes do in outbursts, and welcomed an adversary against whose intrusions he had a more legitimate complaint. I was frankly scared, and noticed with relief that two male residents were trotting through the open doorway, attracted by the commotion. They succeeded between them in quieting the man down, and I left all four of them trying to settle down again to a more sober discussion of matters.

I saw Dr. Scoville later in the day and, itching with curiosity of course, mentioned the incident. But he refused to discuss it beyond a word of thanks to me for stepping in. "I quite understand those things," he said, and, opening a metal chart folder, turned to my problems.

I offer these two vignettes of human collapse, not for their own sakes, or even as necessarily vital links in the narrative, but as preliminaries to describing the moment—not a very pretty story itself—when I reached the end of my own tether.

One time in that criminal winter, when the lights of Christmas sprouted in a thousand windows and the mercies of Methotrexate were drawing to a close, we went in for our fifth hospitalization. Now we were to have our horizons widened. Anterior bleeding is not so bad, but posterior calls for cauterization, as well as packing, back into the throat. "Oh, Daddy, I can't stand it," said my spattered burden as I carried her from the treatment room back to bed. It is one of the few cries of protest I ever heard from the thoroughbred, of whom I bear true and faithful witness. The stigmata were fresh: the wound in the breast from a new aspiration, the prints in the hands from the intravenous and transfusion needles to which the arms were once again spread as she watched television with a reassembled smile. On the screen were unfolding again a few reels of the dear old clowns. The comic for whom rolling 'em in the aisles had been sufficient was doing the narrating, only this time on the side of the intellectuals.

"You see, Daddy? How they wait for the pie, then take their time wiping it off and all? A ritual. He calls it that too."

Stein and his Rachel were not here this time, but the Great Debate went forward between two voices now scarcely for a moment silent in my brain.

"I ask, my Lord, permission to despair."

"On what grounds?"

"The fairy is now a troll. The spine is gone. She supports herself on her breastbone."

"Do you do as well?"

"Do you exist?"

"If I say yes, it will only be as a voice in your mind. Make me say it then, and be quiet."

"Are God and Herod then one?"

"What do you mean?"

"The Slaughter of the Innocents. Who creates a perfect blossom to crush it? Children dying in this building, mice in the next. It's all the same to Him who marks the sparrow's fall."

"I forgive you."

"I cannot say the same. . . . I do not ask that she be spared to me, but that her life be spared to her. Or give us a year. We will spend it as we have the last, missing nothing. We will mark the dance of every hour between the snowdrop and the snow: crocus to tulip to violet to iris to rose. We will note not only the azalea's crimson flowers but the red halo that encircles a while the azalea's root when her petals are shed, also the white halo that rings for a week the foot of the old catalpa tree. Later we will prize the chrysanthemums which last so long; almost as long as paper flowers, perhaps because they know in blooming not to bloom. We will seek out the leaves turning in the little-praised bushes and the unadvertised trees. Everyone loves the sweet, neat blossom of the hawthorn in spring, but who lingers over the olive drab of her leaf in autumn? We will. We will note the lost yellows in the tangles of that bush that spills over the Howards' stone wall, the meek hues among which it seems to hesitate before committing itself to red, and next year learn its name. We will seek out these modest subtleties so lost in the blare of oaks and maples, like flutes and wood-winds drowned in brasses and drums. When winter comes, we will let no snow fall ignored. We will again watch the first blizzard from her window like figures locked snug in a glass paperweight. 'Pick one out and follow it to the ground!' she will say again. We will feed the plain birds that stay to cheer us through the winter, and when spring returns we shall be the first out, to catch the snow-drop's first white whisper in the wood. All this we ask, with the remission of our sins, in Christ's name. Amen." . . .

I stood a while over the quietly breathing child. She had her wig off, and now without her hair I could see how perfectly shaped her head was. Child of the pure, unclouded brow. . . . The stigmata were more marked than ever, those in the hands dark and numerous from many needles, the wound in the breast fresh under its cotton pad. The short strip of adhesive tape over the cotton bore its usual gold star, given for good behavior and valor under fire.

As I stood there, I sensed the door being quietly opened. Turning, I saw the face of Dr. Romulo, the young Filipino resident, thrust shyly into the room. He beckoned me out into the corridor. He took my arm and led me off a few steps. His face had the solemn expression of one bearing important news.

"We just got the marrow report back," he said. "It's down to six per cent. Practically normal. Carol's in remission. . . ."

After parking the car in New York, I picked the boxed cake up carefully from the seat and, pushing the door shut with my knee, carried it down the street. A short distance up ahead I could see Mrs. Morano, the night nurse, turn into the church of St. Catherine for her morning prayers. I shifted the package to one hand in order to open the door. I walked to the front of the church, which had its normal smattering of worshipers. I set the cake down on an empty pew and joined the kneeling figures.

When I rose, Mrs. Morano was standing at the edge of the chancel. We whispered together a moment in greeting as we moved up the aisle.

"You heard about Carol," I said.

"Yes, it's exciting. That's why I'm so sorry about this."

"What?"

"The infection. It's been going through the ward like wildfire. Half of the kids are in oxygen tents."

"Carol?"

She nodded. "They had me phone you this morning, but you'd left. The new drug does depress the white count so terribly, of course, and leave them wide open to infection. It's the old story; you can pick anything up in a hos-pital."

"Staph?"

"I don't know They took a blood culture, but it takes a while for the or-ganisms to grow out. They're putting Chloromycetin into her, I think. Maybe you'd better go up.

I hurried into the hospital. One look at Carol and I knew it was time to say good-by. The invading germ, or germs, had not only ravaged her bloodstream by now, but had broken out on her body surface in septicemic discolorations. Her foul enemy had his will of her well at last. One of the blotches covered where they were trying to insert a catheter, and spread down along a thigh. By afternoon it had traveled to the knee, and by the next, gangrened. Dr. Scoville could not have been kinder.

"Someone has ordered another tank of oxygen," he told me that afternoon in the corridor, "but I think you'll agree it won't be necessary. . . . Well, hello there, Randy, you're going home today." Up, up, my head, for the sake of that childhood whom there is none in heaven to love, and none to love on earth so much as you. Up, up! "I've left orders for all the morphine she needs. She'll slip away quietly. She doesn't know us now. It's just as well, because there isn't much in the new drug, if it's any consolation. We have a cooperative study on it, and the remissions are few and brief, and suspect because of the incidence of Meticorten administered with it. We can never be sure it wasn't the Meticorten in this case. It would only have meant another short reprieve—no pardon." He sighed and went his busy way, to the ends of the earth.

I went back into the room. The nurse was taking her blood pressure. "Almost none at all," she whispered. "It's just as well. Only a matter of hours now at the most." . . . The hands were free of needles now, spread out quietly on the counterpane, with their stigmata to which no more would be added. Her breathing slowed, each breath like a caught sob. But once she smiled a little, and, bending closer, I heard her call something to a comrade on another bicycle. They were flying home from school together, down the hill. "All her dreams are pleasant," the nurse murmured. I was thinking of a line of old poetry. "Death loves a shining mark." Now the flower-stem veins were broken, the flower-stalk of the spine destroyed. But through the troll I saw the fairy still, on her flying wheels, the sun in her hair and in the twinkling spokes. I had seen her practicing the piano in her leotard, there were so many things to do and so little time to do them in. I remembered how little labor the sprite had given her mother, so eager was she to be born, so impatient To Be.

The nurse stepped outside a moment, and I moved quickly from the foot of the bed around to the side, whispering rapidly in our moment alone:

"The Lord bless thee, and keep thee: The Lord make his face shine upon thee, and be gracious unto thee: The Lord lift up his countenance upon thee, and give thee peace."

Then I touched the stigmata one by one: the prints of the needles, the wound in the breast that had for so many months now scarcely ever closed. I caressed the perfectly shaped head. I bent to kiss the cheeks, the breasts that would now never be fulfilled, that no youth would ever touch. "Oh, my lamb."

The lips curled in another smile, one whose secret I thought I knew. I recognized it without the aid of the gaze, now sealed forever from mine, with which it had come to me so often throughout her childhood. It was the expression on her face when her homework was going well, the shine of pride at a column of figures mastered or a poem to spring successfully forged. It was the smile of satisfaction worn at the piano when a new composition had been memorized, on her bicycle when, gripping its vanquished horns, she had ridden past me on her first successful solo around the yard. Sometimes, as on that Saturday morning, she would turn the smile shyly toward me, taking added pleasure in my approval.

But this time the experience was not to be shared. She was going alone. Even without the eyes to help communicate it, there was a glow of the most intense concentration on her face, with that wariness of error or shortcoming that had always made it so complete and so characteristic. She had never seemed more alive than now, when she was gathering all the life within her for the proper discharge of whatever this last assignment might have been. Was it a sum of figures or a poem to nature she was undertaking in her dream? Or a difficult, delicate spray of notes, or the first ecstatic journey on the two-wheeler, with the promise of liberty on summer roads unfolding far ahead? I bent again to whisper a question in her ear, but there was no answer—only the most remote sense of flight upon the face. It shone like a star about to burst and, in bursting, yield me all its light at once could I but bear the gift.

Even her wearied limbs had for the moment this tension, a vibrancy as of a drawn bow. But as the hours wore on, they seemed to slacken, and her features to relax as well. Perhaps the mission had been accomplished, and the hour of rest was at hand. Once, later that afternoon, the smile parted her lips again, this time widely enough to show that her gums were dripping. The enemy was pouring out of every crevice at last. The sight of these royal children pitted against this bestiality had always consumed me with a fury so blind I had had often to turn my face away. Now I was glad Carol could not see me standing there, alone, at last, on holy ground.

She went her way in the middle of the afternoon, borne from the dull watchers on a wave that broke and crashed beyond our sight. In that fathomless and timeless silence one does look rather wildly about for a clock, in a last attempt to fix the lost spirit in time. I had guessed what the hands would say. Three o'clock. The children were putting their schoolbooks away, and getting ready to go home.

After some legal formalities I went into the room once more to say goodby. I had once read a book in which the hero had complained, in a similar farewell taken of a woman, that it was like saying good-by to a statue. I wished it were so now. She looked finally like some mangled flower, or like a bird that had been pelted to earth in a storm. I knew that under the sheet she would look as though she had been clubbed to death. As for the dignity of man, this one drew forth a square of cloth, and, after honking like a goose, pocketed his tears.

The bartender had finished cleaning up after some last late lunchers and was polishing the glasses for the evening's trade. After I'd had six or seven drinks, he said to me, "No more. That must be the tenth muddler you've snapped in two." Perhaps he was hearing the voices too. . . .

Passing the church of St. Catherine on the way to the car, I suddenly remembered the cake. I went inside, out of curiosity. It was still there on the pew, undisturbed. I picked it up and started out with it. An incoming worshiper took frowning note of my unsteady career through the lobby door.

Outside, I paused on the sidewalk, one foot on the bottom step. I turned and looked up at the Figure still hanging as ever over the central doorway, its arms outspread among the sooted stones and strutting doves.

I took the cake out of the box and balanced it a moment on the palm of my hand. Disturbed by something in the motion, the birds started from their covert and flapped away across the street. Then my arm drew back and let fly with all the strength within me. Before the mind snaps, or the heart breaks, it gathers itself like a clock about to strike. It might even be said one pulls himself together to disintegrate. The scattered particles of self—love, wood thrush calling, homework sums, broken nerves, rag dolls, one Phi Beta Kappa key, gold stars, lamplight smiles, night cries, and the shambles of contemplation—are collected for a split moment like scraps of shrapnel before they explode.

It was miracle enough that the pastry should reach its target at all, at that height from the sidewalk. The more so that it should land squarely, just beneath the crown of thorns. Then through scalded eyes I seemed to see the hands free themselves of the nails and move slowly toward the soiled face. Very slowly, very deliberately, with infinite patience, the icing was wiped from the eyes and flung away: I could see it fall in clumps to the porch steps. Then the cheeks were wiped down with the same sense of grave and gentle ritual, with all the kind sobriety of one whose voice could be heard saying, "Suffer the little children to come unto me . . . for of such is the kingdom of heaven."

Then the scene dissolved itself in a mist in which my legs could no longer support their weight, and I sank down to the steps. I sat on its worn stones, to rest a moment before going on. Thus Wanderhope was found at that place which for the diabolists of his literary youth, and for those with more modest spiritual histories too, was said to be the only alternative to the muzzle of a pistol: the foot of the Cross.

# 5. THE USES OF RITUAL

*If we cease to remember our parents, we have no right to expect our children to remember us. In his 1965 reflection on the Jewish practice of saying Kaddish for the dead, Milton Himmelfarb describes the understanding that came to him while performing the prescribed ritual for eleven months after the death of his father. For the Jewish people particularly, with their sense of an unbroken covenant made between God and his chosen people, there is a strong intuition of the links with the dead reaching back in a chain thousands of years. But for everyone, there is a use of ritual by which we find our place, take our place, and finally surrender our place in the passing of generations.*

# Milton Himmelfarb, "Going to Shul"

In the past months, since my father died, I have been in the synagogue twice a day to say the Kaddish. Other congregations would regard mine as observing bankers' hours, but even so its morning schedule requires arising in the dark and cold, especially in the winter. For afternoon-and-evening prayer, the hour varies, depending—at least in principle and in Orthodox synagogues—on the time of sunset, but going every evening is not easy either.

Which is why not even the devout necessarily frequent the synagogue every day, contenting themselves with private prayer, particularly on weekdays. It is the man who is saying the Kaddish who must have a minyan, public worship. In most American synagogues, nearly everyone you see at prayer during the week is a mourner, together with most of those who are there from the beginning on Saturday morning. Inconvenience also helps to explain the tenth-man problem, quite apart from the big explanations we like better: the difficulty of belief, the difficulty of prayer. In few synagogues where the speech is English is it unnecessary to have a list of volunteers who can be telephoned in an emergency to round out the required number of ten.

In the Middle Ages it was thought that saying the Kaddish for a year was especially helpful to the dead if they had been wicked. Since no one wanted to imply that his father or mother had been wicked, today we say the Kaddish for eleven months. I do not know what proportion of Jewish men observe the full eleven months, but I suspect it is fairly high, especially when put beside our known propensity for staying away from the synagogue.

If this is so, why? Well, feelings about death, especially the death of a parent; guilt and anxiety, and the need to relieve them; ritual—all these can be interpreted along conventional Freudian lines and have been, often. For Freud, religion was a kind of public, collective neurosis. I take this idea seriously. It tells me better than anything else why the very inconvenience of saying the Kaddish morning and afternoon or evening every day for eleven months, and thereafter on anniversaries—normally at least two in a man's life—becomes a virtue, perhaps an attraction. It is expiatory, it is almost punitive, and we have been taught that guilt seeks punishment.

It is more, of course. Much has been said in dispraise of Jews who obey the rules of the Kaddish though otherwise they hardly ever pray at all. The contempt is unwarranted: the Kaddish must meet their needs better than anything else in the synagogue. And these are not only needs of the kind we have learned about from Freud, but also needs for style and tradition. Freud said that the collective neurosis of religion spares us the trouble of developing individual, personal neuroses. With the Kaddish, Judaism spares each the trouble of developing for himself a style—etiquette, ritual, mode of expression, symbolic action—at a time when he wants it and when he knows he cannot devise something personal that will be as good.

If each of us were accountable for his own ritual of mourning, who would escape censure? Who would escape his own censure? The Jewish rites—the burial, the seven days at home, the Kaddish—have the advantage of being a tradition, a style. We need assume no responsibility for them, as we would for any personal or private symbolic action, nor can there be any question of their appropriateness. They are appropriate almost by definition, because of their antiquity, their near-universality, their publicness—*quod semper, quod ubique, quod ad omnibus.* Yet their publicness, so far from making them exterior and impersonal, makes them all the more appropriate to the particular relationship between mourner and mourned: the Kaddish I now say for my father, he said for his; and so back through a recession of the generations that exceeds what my imagination can grasp. Acting as my father acted, I become conscious that I am a link in the chain of being. Nor am I hindered from expressing particular, local, present emotion.

One of the things a mourner is supposed to say about someone who has died is the prayer that Abigail said for David (though in his lifetime and in his presence), that his soul may be bound up in the bundle of life. Saying this is of a piece with the rest of our ritual. Whatever its efficacy may be for the dead, it binds me up in the bundle of life, situates me in the procession of the generations, frees me from the prison of now and here.

Although we have been born when it is hard to believe in immortality, the Kaddish helps us to believe, a little. I know that it makes me think of my father often, more than twice a day; and it will keep reminding me of him after I have stopped saying the Kaddish daily, when I hear someone else say it and I make the appropriate response. To think of my father, to recall him, is to hold off his mortality—and because ritual is eloquent, to hold it off still one generation further. Where has Daddy gone? To shul, to say Kaddish for Grandpa. By doing what allows my children to ask this question and receive this answer, I also allow myself to hope that my own mortality will similarly be delayed.

# 6. REFUSING CONSOLATION

*Hundreds of poems, letters of sympathy, and philosophical essays assure us of the possibility of consolation for grief. But across them all, like a jagged line, runs a literature of the refusal of consolation. In poetry particularly, from such ancient poets as Horace (65–8 B.C.) to such twentieth-century poets as Dylan Thomas, there is a tradition of elegy, threnody, and lament that sees any consolation for grief as a betrayal of the dead, an allowing of them to slip away forever. Jody Bottum, poetry editor at* First Things, *assembles this anti-consolation literature to argue that one of the most common notions offered as consolation—the suggestion that death is universal, that everyone must die—results in a "second killing" of the dead. Though we may fail at it, he argues, moral considerations demand a never-ending grief.*

# Jody Bottum, "All That Lives Must Die"

"Good Hamlet," begs his mother at the audience's first sight of the black-clothed prince, "cast thy nighted color off,"

> And let thine eye look like a friend on Denmark.
> Do not forever with thy lids
> Seek for thy noble father in the dust.
> Thou know'st 'tis common; all that lives must die,
> Passing through nature to eternity.
> *Hamlet:*　Aye, Madam, 'tis common.
> *Gertrude:*　If it be,
> 　Why seems it so particular with thee?

The scene is rich with the play of language, as scenes in Shakespeare always are. Hamlet agrees that death is common, meaning the opposite of noble, but Gertrude had said that death is common, meaning the opposite of particular. . . . So too this second scene in *Hamlet* is rich with themes the play will later develop: the newly re-married Queen's embarrassment before the still-grieving Prince; her new husband's uneasy possession of the throne; her kittenish tendency—the impulse of the aging coquette—to please and comfort men; perhaps even her genuine and loving wish to see her son consoled. And yet, though Gertrude has complex reasons to want an end to Hamlet's public mourning, her actual argument is simple: recollecting at last our knowledge that death is "common," remembering at length our certainty that "all that lives must die," we ought to leave off weeping.

The new King Claudius, too, and for equally complex reasons, seeks an end to Hamlet's mourning. "You must know, your father lost a father," he continues his wife's argument, "That father lost, lost his." Reflection ought to bring to mind the "common theme" of nature: not just that fathers die, but that fathers *must* die:

> To persevere
> In obstinate condolment is a course
> Of impious stubbornness; 'tis unmanly grief,
> It shows a will most incorrect to heaven,
> A heart unfortified, a mind impatient,
> An understanding simple and unschool'd.
> For what we know must be and is as common

As any the most vulgar thing to sense.
Why should we in our peevish opposition
Take it to heart? Fie! 'Tis a fault to heaven,
A fault against the dead, a fault to nature,
To reason most absurd, whose common theme
Is death of fathers, and who still hath cried,
From the first corpse till he that died today,
"This must be so."

Hamlet, of course, is not consoled—as the audience knows he surely ought not to be. Claudius, seeking some expression for the universality of death, lights on the obvious trope, "From the first corpse till he that died today." But the first corpse was Abel, murdered by his brother, and the most recent corpse is Hamlet's father, also murdered by a brother. Claudius—in the manner Freud enjoined us to watch for in Shakespeare—unconsciously confesses his guilt even as he tries to check the grief of the last mourner for his victim.

Something more, however, than merely guilty motives is wrong with the argument Gertrude and Claudius offer Hamlet. The fact that Shakespeare puts it in the mouths of the guilty pair shows, I think, his awareness of the consolation's weakness. What help, after all, is "This must be so"? Who tries to console a child for her broken doll by telling her that all dolls break, it's what dolls do? Offered as a consolation, death's universality would be comic were it not so sad. What could a child feel at being assured that not only has her old doll broken, but so will every other doll she owns? And what compulsion can we use when she does not take the notion as consoling? Knowledge of universal death ought logically to make grief worse, not better: not only has my father died, but so will everyone I ever love.

The world is full of theories about *Hamlet,* but one theory I find helpful claims that the play in part presents the revulsion of medieval Christianity at the Renaissance revival of pagan philosophy. Neoplatonism and Aristotelianism, the major schools of ancient philosophy, survived throughout the Middle Ages and had been reconciled to some degree with Christian theology. But the Renaissance rediscovered the minor, unassimilated schools of ancient pagan thought: Cynicism, Epicureanism, Skepticism, and, especially, Stoicism. Indeed, from Shakespeare's time through the nineteenth century, "philosophical" meant in English primarily what in the twentieth century we would call "stoical." The woolly arguments of Gertrude and Claudius are thus not new, but merely bad examples of a general revival that marks Renaissance thought. And in our preference for the grief of Hamlet above the consolation of Gertrude and Claudius, Shakespeare shows us something of the problem created by this Renaissance revival.

Hamlet is no saintly Christian: "Now could I drink hot blood," he swears. And Claudius is no grave and noble Roman Stoic: a murderer, carouser, plotter, and seducer of his brother's wife, he could never have been "philosophical" in the stoical sense of the word—never have hidden his fright when the play within the play manages "to catch the conscience of the King," never have proven in suicide "more an antique Roman than a Dane." But the clash between them may nonetheless be in part a clash between Christianity and Stoicism, for Hamlet's mind moves in a way that St. Augustine would recognize and Claudius' mind in a way that Seneca would know. It takes a Christian, albeit a bad one, to hesitate to kill a kneeling man—as Hamlet hesitates to kill Claudius—for fear that, slain at prayer, the victim escape hell-fire. It takes a Stoic, albeit a bad one, to urge his murder victim's son to contemplate the naturalness of death. The irony of Claudius' argument for consolation deserves notice: Who better to trust than a murderer for the news that all men die?

Some awareness of a clash between Christianity and Stoicism in the play gives us an insight into the oddity of being consoled by death's universality: To take solace for the death of one human being in the fact that all human beings die is on its face absurd or even spiteful. But the logical invalidity of a consolation does not prevent it from being in fact psychologically consoling, and there is, as the Stoics saw, a way in which universal death may actually console us for a particular death. Hamlet's problem and ours as well, is that this Stoical way of consoling grief ends in a denial of the reality of the dead person for whom the mourner grieves—a denial Gertrude and Claudius undoubtedly desire. . . .

Our knowledge of the impermanence of things is itself a sort of permanence. We comprehend a deathless unity when we observe the dying multiplicity; when we contemplate the stream of time, we transcend death in thought: thinking of our span of days, and thus supposing we shall exist beyond them. It seemed to the Stoics that this fact might be used for consolation. Only if nothing were to die may we banish grief. But since things do die, the only way to say they do not is to emphasize the fact they do. This is less paradoxical than it sounds. There is a consolation in the universal, for the ability to think of death implies the thinker stands above that death. In that horrifying letter in which he urges a dying man to think about death, Seneca means to be consoling: the more we emphasize death and destruction, the more we will rise above them; the more we think on death and destruction, the less real they will become. When the Stoic says that all men die, he means that they do not.

The gain of this Stoic *memento mori,* however, is purchased at a cost: not only does death become less real, but so do the particular things that die. In his struggle to keep alive the memory of his father that everyone else at Denmark's court seems so willing to let go, Hamlet sees what all who have ever grieved must see: Knowledge of universal death cannot console us for the fact that a real, unique, and particular person has been ripped from being, that a hole exists in the fabric of the universe, that all the real possibilities which once depended upon that dead person are now no longer possible.

There is, of course, a remedy for grief in "the long lapse of time," as Cicero writes, "slow-working it is true but effectual." And yet, he adds, "it is not the mere lapse of time that produces this effect, but continued reflection. For if the circumstances are the same, and the person is the same, how can there be any change in the grief felt?" Our experience certainly is that grief weakens in time; indeed, in *Mourning and Melancholia* Freud describes grief as a form of insanity that we do not bother to treat as insane because we are confident that it will pass. But this, as Cicero sees, is exactly the problem. The passage of time, taken by itself, cannot be what dilutes our grief, for the cause of that grief remains untouched by time: the real person whom we really loved is just as dead and gone. Grief must be drowned, rather, by some event that happens in that passage of time.

For Cicero, this event is a slow but inevitable re-emergence of rationality. "There is no grief that is not diminished and mitigated by the lapse of years," Sulpicius reminds him when Cicero himself seemed to over-mourn his daughter's early death; "To await that lapse, instead of hastening to forestall the effect by applying your wisdom, is not creditable to you." For Freud, too, time brings about a rationalization in which we accept the world of possibilities as actually constituted—in which we no longer seek the impossible object but become sane once again.

But what right has grief to grow so thin? "Let love clasp grief lest both be drowned," Tennyson demands in *In Memoriam*, "Let darkness keep her raven gloss." We do a disservice to the dead when we accept and rationalize in abstraction the fact of death. We forget the life that was, we kill the corpse a second time, when we abandon grief's struggle to maintain the always present absence of the beloved dead person whom we mourn. . . .

It is true that, insensibly, we do in fact let the dead slip away. . . . And it is true that the world does in fact go on in spite of grief. But neither of these facts makes it right that we forget or ever cease to grieve. The first guilt felt in grief is that the guilty lover dares to live, even in grief; the second guilt is that the lover dares to live even after grief has ceased. Gradually, in care for other things, in the wants and the needs of the body, perhaps even in the burden of charity, the bustle draws us back and we cease at length to grieve. And one bright day, we notice that we have ceased to grieve, and all the world goes black in guilty grief again. But the inwardness of grief decays and we find it harder and harder to summon up the ghostly present absence of the dead. C. S. Lewis, in his painstaking self-scrutiny after the death of his wife, observes the strange sharp guilt that accompanies the first awareness of having been for a moment not grieving—the guilt that accompanies the knowledge that grief is dying.

This guilt has always seemed to me to reflect a genuine moral impulse. The reminder that death is common—that all that lives must die—may remind us that we lack the strength and time to grieve for all the dead. . . . But that we must fail to grieve for all provides no reason to cease to grieve for some. I do not know all the dead, but those dead whom I know depend in some important way upon my grief. . . . Grief does seem to fade despite the guilt we feel as it does, as Cicero and Freud both saw. But its fading ought to be a cause for deep suspicion to a moral imagination. . . . Unless the dead will stand again before us as themselves—unless death is in fact unreal—grief ought rightly never end. And "the immortality of souls brings us not the slightest consolation," as Fronto observes in a letter to Marcus Aurelius. "Be the immortality of the soul ever so established, that will be a theme for the disputations of philosophers, it will never assuage the yearning of a parent."

According to some interpretations of *Hamlet,* the Prince's obstinate grief may have conjured or projected the ghost upon the Danish battlements, for he can find even a troubled consolation only in actual sight of his father. . . . A clear reading of *Hamlet,* a clear reading of ourselves, requires that we not lie to ourselves about this, any more than Hamlet does—though his honesty on this one point drives him nearly mad and forces him to a dozen other self-deceptions. Short of the immediate opening of the graves—short of resurrection *now*—there is no consolation: only the vilest of abstractions and the most self-serving of forgettings.

# 7. THE LIFE OF THE WORLD TO COME

*The greatest collection of biblical readings on death and hope and judgment and resurrection is the Christian burial service, developed over many centuries of Church history.* The Book of Common Prayer *is the service book used in the Church of England and other churches of the Anglican communion. The first Prayer Book (1549), mainly the work of Thomas Cranmer, was revised and made compulsory in England by the Act of Uniformity (1662). The first U.S. revision was adopted by the Episcopal Church in 1789; the text given here is taken from the 1928 edition.* The Book of Common Prayer *has influenced the liturgies of other churches and is undoubtedly among the most beautiful and best-known texts in the English language. In the Christian burial of the dead, with its readings from the Psalms, St. Paul's first Epistle to the Corinthians, and many other biblical texts, most of the classic themes of death are gathered together and given a timeless exposition. There is hope and sorrow, memory and healing, an acknowledgment of loss and a promise of life eternal.*

# The Book of Common Prayer

## The Order for the Burial of the Dead

*The Minister, meeting the Body, and going before it shall say or sing:*

I am the resurrection and the life, saith the Lord: he that believeth in me, though he were dead, yet shall he live: and whosoever liveth and believeth in me, shall never die.

I know that my redeemer liveth, and that he shall stand at the latter day upon the earth: and though this body be destroyed, yet shall I see God: whom I shall see for myself, and mine eyes shall behold, and not as a stranger.

We brought nothing into this world, and it is certain we can carry nothing out. The Lord gave, and the Lord hath taken away; blessed be the name of the Lord.

*After they are come into the Church, shall be said the following selections, taken from the Psalms.*

Lord, let me know mine end, and the number of my days; that I may be certified how long I have to live.

Behold, thou hast made my days as it were a span long, and mine age is even as nothing in respect of thee; and verily every man living is altogether vanity.

For man walketh in a vain shadow, and disquieteth himself in vain; he heapeth up riches, and cannot tell who shall gather them.

And now, Lord, what is my hope? truly my hope is even in thee.

Deliver me from all mine offences; and make me not a rebuke unto the foolish.

When thou with rebukes dost chasten man for sin, thou makest his beauty to consume away, like as it were a moth fretting a garment: every man therefore is but vanity.

Hear my prayer, O Lord, and with thine ears consider my calling; hold not thy peace at my tears;

For I am a stranger with thee, and a sojourner, as all my fathers were.

O spare me a little, that I may recover my strength, before I go hence, and be no more seen. (Psalm 69)

Lord, thou hast been our refuge, from one generation to another.

Before the mountains were brought forth, or ever the earth and the world were made, thou art God from everlasting, and world without end.

Thou turnest man to destruction; again thou sayest, Come again, ye children of men.

For a thousand years in thy sight are but as yesterday, when it is past, and as a watch in the night.

As soon as thou scatterest them they are even as a sleep; and fade away suddenly like the grass.

In the morning it is green, and groweth up; but in the evening it is cut down, dried up, and withered.

For we consume away in thy displeasure, and are afraid at thy wrathful indignation.

Thou hast set our misdeeds before thee; and our secret sins in the light of thy countenance.

For when thou art angry all our days are gone: we bring our years to an end, as it were a tale that is told.

The days of our age are threescore years and ten; and though men be so strong that they come to fourscore years, yet is their strength then but labour and sorrow; so soon passeth it away, and we are gone.

So teach us to number our days, that we may apply our hearts unto wisdom. (Psalm 90)


I will lift up mine eyes unto the hills; from whence cometh my help?

My help cometh even from the Lord, who hath made heaven and earth.

He will not suffer thy foot to be moved; and he that keepeth thee will not sleep.

Behold, he that keepeth Israel shall neither slumber nor sleep.

The Lord himself is thy keeper; the Lord is thy defense upon thy right hand;

So that the sun shall not burn thee by day, neither the moon by night.

The Lord shall preserve thee from all evil; yea, it is even he that shall keep thy soul.

The Lord shall preserve thy going out, and thy coming in, from this time forth for evermore. (Psalm 121)


Out of the deep have I called unto thee, O Lord; Lord, hear my voice.

O let thine ears consider well the voice of my complaint.

If thou, Lord, wilt be extreme to mark what is done amiss, O Lord, who may abide it?

For there is mercy with thee; therefore shalt thou be feared.

I look for the Lord; my soul doth wait for him; in his word is my trust.

My soul fleeth unto the Lord before the morning watch; I say, before the morning watch.

O Israel, trust in the Lord, for with the Lord there is mercy, and with him is plenteous redemption.

And he shall redeem Israel from all his sins. (Psalm 130)

*Then shall follow the Lesson, taken out of the fifteenth chapter of the first Epistle of St. Paul to the Corinthians.*

Now is Christ risen from the dead, and become the firstfruits of them that slept. For since by man came death, by man came also the resurrection of the dead. For as in Adam all die, even so in Christ shall all be made alive. But every man in his own order: Christ the firstfruits; afterward they that are Christ's at his coming. Then cometh the end, when he shall have delivered up the kingdom to God, even the Father; when he shall have put down all rule and all authority and power. For he must reign, till he hath put all enemies under his feet. The last enemy that shall be destroyed is death. For he hath put all things under his feet. But when he saith all things are put under him, it is manifest that he is excepted, which did put all things under him. And when all things shall be subdued unto him, then shall the Son also himself be subject unto him that put all things under him, that God may be all in all. But some man will say, How are the dead raised up? and with what body do they come? Thou foolish one, that which thou sowest is not quickened, except it die: and that which thou sowest, thou sowest not that body that shall be, but bare grain, it may chance of wheat, or of some other grain: but God giveth it a body as it hath pleased him, and to every seed its own body.

All flesh is not the same flesh: but there is one kind of flesh of men, another flesh of beasts, another of fishes, and another of birds. There are also celestial bodies, and bodies terrestrial: but the glory of the celestial is one, and the glory of the terrestrial is another. There is one glory of the sun, and another glory of the moon, and another glory of the stars: for one star differeth from another star in glory. So also is the resurrection of the dead. It is sown in corruption; it is raised in incorruption: it is sown in dishonor; it is raised in glory: it is sown in weakness; it is raised in power: it is sown a natural body; it is raised a spiritual body. There is a natural body, and there is a spiritual body. And so it is written, The first man Adam was made a living soul; the last Adam was made a quickening spirit. Howbeit that was not first which is spiritual, but that which is natural; and afterward that which is spiritual. The first man is of the earth, earthy: the second man is the Lord from heaven. As is the earthy, such are they also that are earthy: and as is the heavenly, such are they also that are heavenly. And as we have borne the image of the earthy, we shall also bear the image of the heavenly.

Now this I say, brethren, that flesh and blood cannot inherit the kingdom of God; neither doth corruption inherit incorruption. Behold, I shew you a mystery; We shall not all sleep, but we shall all be changed, in a moment, in the twinkling of an eye, at the last trump: for the trumpet shall sound, and the dead shall be raised incorruptible, and we shall be changed. For this corruptible must put on incorruption, and this mortal must put on immortality. So when this corruptible shall have put on incorruption, and this mortal shall have put on immortality, then shall be brought to pass the saying that is written, Death is swallowed up in victory. O death, where is thy sting? O grave, where is thy victory? The sting of death is sin; and the strength of sin is the law. But thanks be to God, which giveth us the victory through our Lord Jesus Christ. Therefore, my beloved brethren, be ye steadfast, unmoveable, always abounding in the work of the Lord, forasmuch as ye know that your labor is not in vain in the Lord.

*Here may be sung a Hymn or Anthem; and, at the discretion of the Minister, the Creed, the Lord's Prayer, the Prayer which followeth, and such other fitting Prayers, ending with the Blessing; the Minister, before the Prayers, first pronouncing,*

Remember thy servant, O Lord, according to the favor which thou bearest unto thy people, and grant that, increasing in knowledge and love of thee, he may go from strength to strength, in the life of perfect service, in thy heavenly kingdom; through Jesus Christ our Lord, who liveth and reigneth with thee and the Holy Ghost ever, one God, world without end. Amen.

Unto God's gracious mercy and protection we commit you. The Lord bless you and keep you, The Lord make his face to shine upon you, and be gracious unto you. The Lord lift up his countenance upon you, and give you peace, both now and evermore. Amen.

*When they come to the Grave, while the Body is made ready to be laid into the earth, shall be sung or said,*

Man, that is born of a woman, hath but a short time to live, and is full of misery. He cometh up, and is cut down, like a flower; he fleeth as it were a shadow, and never continueth in one stay. In the midst of life we are in death; of whom may we seek for succor, but of thee, O Lord, who for our sins art justly displeased? Yet, O Lord God most holy, O Lord most mighty, O holy and most merciful Savior, deliver us not into the bitter pains of eternal death. Thou knowest, Lord, the secrets of our hearts; shut not thy merciful ears to our prayer; but spare us, Lord most holy, O God most mighty, O holy and merciful Savior, thou most worthy Judge eternal, suffer us not, at our last hour, for any pains of death, to fall from thee.

*Then, while the earth shall be cast upon the Body by some standing by, the Minister shall say,*

Unto Almighty God we commend the soul of our brother (sister) departed, and we commit his body to the ground; earth to earth, ashes to ashes, dust to dust; in sure and certain hope of the Resurrection unto eternal life, through our Lord Jesus Christ; at whose coming in glorious majesty to judge the world, the earth and the sea shall give up their dead; and the corruptible bodies of those who sleep in him shall be changed, and made like unto his own glorious body; according to the mighty working whereby he is able to subdue all things unto himself.

*Then shall be said or sung,*

I heard a voice from heaven, saying unto me, Write, From henceforth blessed are the dead who die in the Lord: even so saith the Spirit; for they rest from their labors. . . .

*Then the Minister shall say,*

Almighty and everliving God, we yield unto thee most high praise and hearty thanks, for the wonderful grace and virtue declared in all thy saints, who have been the choice vessels of thy grace, and the lights of the world in their several generations; most humbly beseeching thee to give us grace so to follow the example of their steadfastness in thy faith, and obedience to thy holy commandments, that at the day of the general Resurrection, we, with all those who are of the mystical body of thy Son, may be set on his right hand, and hear his most joyful voice: Come, ye blessed of my Father, inherit the kingdom prepared for you from the foundation of the world. Grant this, O Father, for the sake of the same, thy Son Jesus Christ, our only Mediator and Advocate. Amen.

# SOURCES AND CREDITS

The editor and the publisher thank the owners of copyright for their permission to include selections within this anthology.

Abernathy, Ralph David. *And the Walls Came Tumbling Down: An Autobiography.* New York: HarperCollins, 1989, pp. 447–50, 456–60, 461–66. © 1989 by Ralph David Abernathy. Reprinted by permission of HarperCollins Publishers, Inc.

Alvarez, A. *The Savage God: A Study of Suicide.* New York: Random House, 1971, pp. 33–41. © 1971 by A. Alvarez. Reprinted with the permission of Gillon Aitken Associates Ltd.

Bandeira, Manuel. "Profundamente," from *This Earth, That Sky,* translated by Candace Slater. Berkeley: University of California Press, 1989. Translation © 1989 Candace Slater. Reprinted by permission.

*The Book of Common Prayer.* "Burial Rite." New York: The Church Pension Fund, 1928.

Bottum, Jody. "All That Lives Must Die." *First Things* 63 (May 1996), pp. 28–32. By permission of *First Things* and the author.

Bowker, John. *The Meanings of Death.* Excerpts on the *Quran.* Cambridge: Cambridge University Press, 1991, pp. 102–128. Reprinted with the permission of Cambridge University Press.

Chergé, Christian de. "Last Testament," translated by the Monks of Mount Saint Bernard Abbey, Leicester, England. *First Things* 65 (August/September 1996). By permission of *First Things.*

De Vries, Peter. *The Blood of the Lamb.* New York: Little, Brown, 1961, pp. 168–238. © 1961 by Peter De Vries. Reprinted with permission of the Estate of Peter De Vries, Derek De Vries, Executor.

Dickens, Charles. *Dombey and Son.* Everyman's Library. New York: Knopf, 1994.

Donne, John. "Meditation XVI, 'Et properare meum clamant,'" in *Devotions Upon Emergent Occasions and Death's Duel.* New York: Vintage, 1999.

Ford, Jeffery E. "Mercy Killing at Golgotha." *First Things* 66 (October 1996), pp. 9–10. By permission of *First Things* and the author.

Herbert, George. "Mortification," in *The Complete English Poems,* edited by James Tobin. New York: Penguin Classics, 1992.

Himmelfarb, Milton. "Going to Shul," in *The Jews of Modernity.* New York: Basic Books, 1973. © 1973 by Basic Books, Inc. Reprinted by permission of Basic Books, a member of Perseus Books, L.L.C.

Islam, Khawaja Muhammad. *The Spectacle of Death: Including Glimpses of Life beyond the Grave.* Excerpts on the *Quran.* Lahore: Tablighi Kutub Khana, 1976. Reprinted as *Spectacle of Death and the Afterlife.* Chicago: KAZI Publications, 1987. Used by permission of KAZI Publications, Inc.

*Katha Upanishad,* in *The Ten Principal Upanishads,* translated by Shree Purohit Swami and W. B. Yeats. Winchester, Mass.: Faber and Faber, 1988.

Lewis, C. S. *A Grief Observed.* San Francisco: HarperSanFrancisco, 1961, pp. 19–32. © 1961 by N. W. Clerk. Reprinted by permission of HarperCollins Publishers, Inc.

Mason, Alane Salierno. "Reconciliation of Unbelief." *Commonweal* (March 22, 1996). © 1996 by Commonweal Foundation. Reprinted with permission of Alane Salierno Mason.

Meilaender, Gilbert. "I Want to Burden My Loved Ones." *First Things* 16 (October 1991), pp. 12–14. By permission of *First Things* and the author.

Montaigne, Michel de. "To Philosophize Is to Learn to Die," in *Essays of Michel de Montaigne,* translated by Charles Cotton. Garden City, N.J.: Doubleday & Co., 1947.

O'Connor, Flannery. "A Good Man Is Hard to Find," from *A Good Man Is Hard to Find and Other Stories.* New York: Harcourt Brace, 1953. © 1953 by Flannery O'Connor and renewed 1981 by Regina O'Connor. Reprinted by permission of Harcourt, Inc.

Owen, Wilfred. "Anthem for Doomed Youth," in *The Collected Poems of Wilfred Owen.* New York: New Directions, 1963.

*The Rubáiyát of Omar Khayyám,* translated by Edward FitzGerald. New York: Doubleday & Co., 1952.

Sandeen, Ernest. "Do Not Go Gentle," from *Can These Bones Live?* Notre Dame, Ind.: University of Notre Dame Press, 1995. Reprinted by permission of the University of Notre Dame Press.

Shakespeare, William. *Henry V.* New Folger Library Shakespeare, edited by Barbara A. Mowat and Paul Werstine. New York: Washington Square Press, 1995.

Thomas, Dylan. "A Refusal to Mourn the Death, by Fire, of a Child in London," from *The Poems of Dylan Thomas,* edited by Daniel Jones. New York: W. W. Norton, 1945. © 1945 by The Trustees for the Copyrights of Dylan Thomas. Reprinted by permission of New Directions Publishing Corp.

Tolstoy, Leo. "The Death of Ivan Ilych," from *The Death of Ivan Ilych and Other Stories,* translated by Louise and Aylmer Maude. Oxford: Oxford University Press, 1935. Reprinted by permission of Oxford University Press.

Von Hildebrand, Dietrich. *Jaws of Death, Gate of Heaven: How to Face Death without Fear.* New York: Sophia Institute Press, 1991, pp. 7–10, 43–44. © 1991 by Sophia Institute Press. Reprinted with permission of Alice Von Hildebrand.

Zaleski, Carol. *The Life of the World to Come: Near Death Experience and Christian Hope: The Albert Cardinal Meyer Lectures.* Oxford: Oxford University Press, 1996, pp. 18–21, 31–36, 69, 76. © 1996 by Carol Zaleski. Used by permission of Oxford University Press, Inc.